PRESERVATION

HALL

PORTRAITS

Frontispiece: Kid Thomas

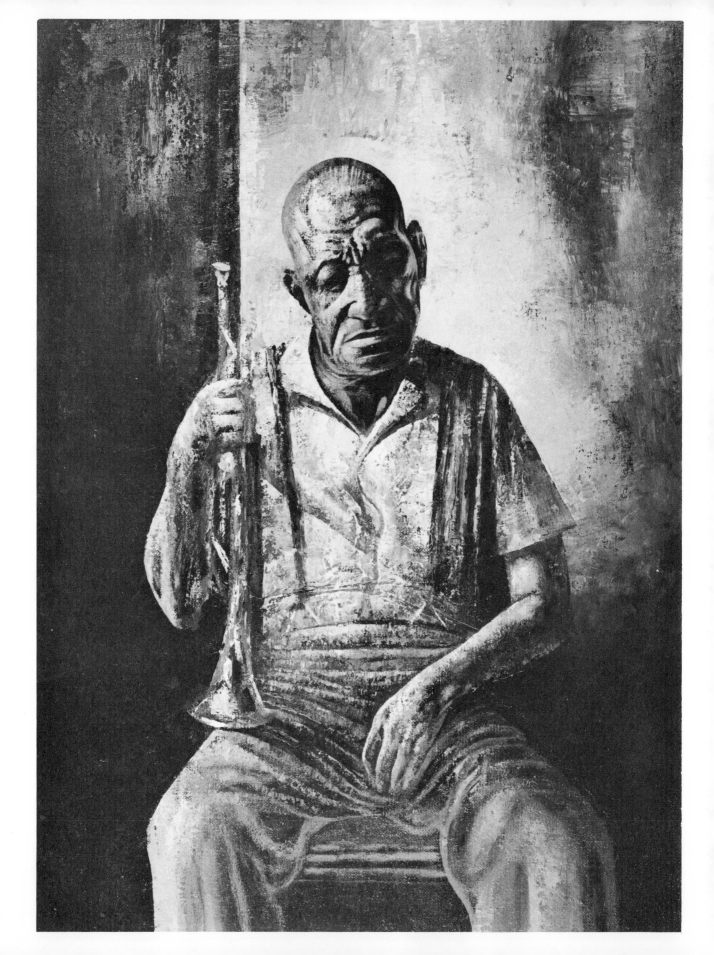

PRESERVATION

Paintings by NOEL ROCKMORE

HALL

Text by LARRY BORENSTEIN

PORTRAITS

and BILL RUSSELL

LOUISIANA STATE UNIVERSITY PRESS · Baton Rouge

Copyright © 1968 by
LOUISIANA STATE UNIVERSITY PRESS

Library of Congress Catalog Card Number: 68-28494

Composition by
Service Typographers, Inc., Indianapolis, Indiana

Printed and Bound by
The Colonial Press, Inc., Clinton, Massachusetts

Designed by Robert L. Nance

Photography by Dan Leyrer, Jules Cahn, and Jack Beech

This book is respectfully dedicated to the spirit and memory of "Papa" John Joseph, who, more than any other, typifies the New Orleans musicians who shared in the Preservation Hall experience. His career was rescued from oblivion at the last possible moment and given a new audience and documentation before the inevitable passing.

E. L. B.

PRESERVATION

HALL

PORTRAITS

INTRODUCTION

Larry Borenstein

Preservation Hall, like the paintings which line its walls, started casually and grew to national prominence. The chain of events is so much the history of my New Orleans gallery that I think I should tell it in the first person.

In 1952 I moved my gallery to 726 St. Peter Street. The building had been occupied by a succession of creative people—Knute Heldner, Pops Whitesell, Erle Stanley Gardner, William Spratling, and others. Its architecture (it was built before 1800 as a Spanish tavern) and its location (next door to Pat O'Brien's) made it ideal for the display and sale of paintings. I coined the name "Associated Artists Studio" and worked cooperatively with the available talents. The location, however, demanded night hours, which interfered with my listening to jazz. I found that by my closing time most bands had knocked off. Occasionally I got to hear Billie and DeDe Pierce at Luthjen's; some weekends I crossed the river to hear Kid Thomas at the Moulin Rouge. But this was not nearly enough music for me, so I bought an old piano and invited the musicians to come to the gallery. I supplied beer and passed a kitty. These sessions— called "rehearsals" to avoid union trouble—were closed; only people I knew or who seemed seriously interested were invited. If music got underway without prearrangement, I phoned friends to pass the word to ensure an audience. Sometimes the musicians divided a few dollars; other times, usually when some generous out-of-towner worked his way in, the rewards were better.

The concerts took place regularly. Punch Miller, back from his long years on the road, brought a band to the gallery Tuesday nights. Kid Thomas had a "rehearsal" every Thursday night, and on Sundays Noon Johnson often stopped by with his trio. Piano "professors" Stormy Weatherly, John Smith, and Isadore Washington often dropped in, as did busking guitarists, banjoists, and harmonica virtuosos. Often impromptu sessions got underway because Lemon Nash dropped in to say "hello" and just happened to have his ukelele with him.

As interest in the music grew, so did resistance. Neighbors who found they could live comfortably with Pat O'Brien's music found ours something to complain about. The police calls became a constant source of apprehension. On two or three occasions the police sent the paddy wagon and jailed everybody. The bands frequently included both white and Negro musicians, and it was simpler to charge them with "disturbing the peace" than with breaking down segregation barriers.

These were changing times in New Orleans and the mood was reflected in night court. A certain judge managed to combine the judicial dignity of a kangaroo court and the philosophy of lynch law with the humor of Milton Berle. An archconservative, the judge was outraged at any racial mixing. When cases of this sort came before him, the courtroom was treated to a tirade on white supremacy spiced with raucous humor and homely philosophy expressed in curbstone epithets. "His Honor" was a mimic and often parodied a defendant. Sometimes he delivered a diatribe if he thought the defendant's hair was too long. On other occasions he would treat the courtroom to an uninhibited dissertation on social ills, and often in the midst of his declamation he would call for order and threaten to clear the courtroom if the laughter which he had provoked was not stilled.

One night in 1957 Kid Thomas and several musicians, white and colored, stood before him. In stern tones the judge delivered a lecture. "We don't want Yankees coming to New Orleans mixing cream with our coffee." He went on to say that Thomas Valentine was well liked by decent folks in nearby Algiers and also appreciated as a "good yard boy." People thought well of him for giving cornet lessons to West Bank kids, and if he would remember his place in the future and not get "uppity," the judge would let him go this time.

The sessions grew in popularity, and so I moved my gallery next door, and the old building was used exclusively for music. Incidentally, no attempt was made, then or since, to fancy up the place. It is a dark, dingy room furnished only with backless wooden benches and a few ancient kitchen chairs. On the average night more than half of the audience has to stand. Some of the floor boards are loose, and the front panel has been knocked out of the old upright piano, in which at least one note is missing.

In 1960 Grayson Mills decided to record Punch Miller. Mills wanted nightly rehearsals with an audience and was surprised to find that the kitty collection enabled him to actually pay the band union scale. This led to an agreement with the musician's union, permitting nightly concerts, and Preservation Hall came out from underground.

A club was formed with the pretentious title of The Society for the Preservation of Traditional New Orleans Jazz. Alas, as in most jazz clubs, there was as much feuding as music. I realized that the only hope was to put the activity on a businesslike basis. The club was dissolved, and Allan and Sandra Jaffe undertook to operate Preservation Hall as a business. They were enthusiastic and willing to take the risks of this unlikely venture. At first it was necessary to subsidize the Hall, and Sandy took a daytime job to help support the nightly concerts. We all hoped that if the music could be presented, a paying audience for it would develop. The kitty policy was continued, but we found that the Hall often filled with people who really didn't care for the music but who would put a few coins in the kitty and stay on because it was quaint and inexpensive. After much soul-searching it was decided that unless a listener was willing to chip in enough to help pay for the band, he should not be admitted.

This in effect established a minimum donation, without which Preservation Hall could not have survived. In practice it is handled with great flexibility. Sandy, an excellent judge of character, frequently invites students, foreigners, musicians, and other persons whom she deems deserving, to come in as guests. On the other hand, she is adamant in her insistence that a donation be given by those who impress her as merely satisfying their curiosity. Of course, most people who come to the Hall genuinely like the music and are glad for an opportunity to help support it.

Another decision concerned requests. Favorites such as "The Saints" and "Tiger Rag" were played several times each night, and lesser known traditional numbers were rarely heard. The now famous request sign was lettered and hung. It reads: "Traditional Requests $1; Others $2; The Saints $5." The number of requests diminished, with the result that the leader could call his own tunes. Usually the leader of a New Orleans band is aware of his audience and knows when to play a vocal, a fast number, or a slow number. This policy change improved the quality of the music.

More than two hundred musicians have played in Preservation Hall since its official opening June 10, 1961—about seventy of them with some regularity. Their ages have ranged from sixty to ninety. Among the bands which alternate are Kid Thomas and his Algiers Stompers, Jim Robinson's New Orleans Band, Kid Shiek and his Storyville Ramblers, Punch Miller's Bunch, Percy Humphrey's Crescent City Joymakers, George Lewis' All Stars, and Billie and DeDe Pierce.

An unexpected byproduct of the sessions in the early fifties was a series of jazz watercolors by Sidney Kittinger. They were vivid impressions executed with a freshness which made them popular with tourists, and they sold readily. Soon other artists—among them Andrew Lang, Harold Quistgard, Joan Farrar, Richard Bell, and Dick Hoffman—came along, and a variety of jazz paintings resulted.

In 1961 I commissioned Xavier de Callatay to do a series of oils of the musicians. Several were done in a pleasing, skillful manner, but they fell short of my expectations as definitive paintings to document the jazzmen. By 1962 I had given up hope that any significant group of paintings would evolve. Just when this goal seemed unattainable, Noel Rockmore returned to New Orleans and did a few sketches. These delighted me. He seemed to plumb the very depths of the souls of the musicians—the pathos, the despair, the heroism, the irony.

Night after night for months Rockmore took up a vantage point in the Hall and painted furiously. Quickly in the dim light, using masonite and polymer, he captured what he heard, what he felt, and what he saw. Polymer, a relatively new acrylic medium, dries immediately, and most painters shun it because it does not allow time to make painting decisions. For Rockmore, this characteristic was an asset. Most of the paintings were accomplished during a thirty-minute set, and it was not unusual for three or four paintings to result from a single night's work. The paintings combined unmistakable likenesses of the musicians, unerring composition, and superb technique. Rockmore selected from the hundreds of sensations that essence which, when set down, permits the viewer to share his experience. He seemed to relish the distractions, and some of the best paintings were produced on the most crowded nights. The audiences at Preservation Hall soon learned that Rockmore took his work seriously. Sometimes a well-meaning tourist would peek over his shoulder, only to be treated as an unwelcome intruder. At closing time Noel gathered up the work and we discussed each piece. Only occasionally did we agree that one should be destroyed.

Each night Rockmore invited one of the musicians to come to his studio the following day to sit for an oil portrait. Appointments were for early afternoon to take advantage of the superb north light. These paintings were completed in two or three hours. Most of the musicians sat for Noel as a favor to me, but after the series got underway the word got out that it was fun to sit for a Rockmore portrait. At first some were hesitant. One had seen a painting of a musician playing a green trombone; another feared that he would look older than he really was. Some complained that Noel made their skin too dark or their faces too sad. Most of them preferred the pleasant, flattering likenesses produced by street hacks who work from photographs, making pretty but patronizing pictures to sell to tourists. A few would not subject themselves to his brush for fear he would not flatter them or because they felt they should have a voice in how they should be posed. As the paintings were framed and hung on the walls of Preservation Hall, however, the musicians looked forward to their turn. Within the space of ten months more than three hundred polymers and about a hundred oils were completed.

The paintings do more than depict those individuals who shared in this jazz revival. They show the bond between the jazzmen and the link of common experience. Since the series has been completed, examples of it have toured the United States, and their unique merit has helped focus attention on Preservation Hall as a part of New Orleans' cultural offering.

I find a curious parallel between Rockmore's jazz paintings and the American Indian paintings of George Catlin. In both instances an artist set out to rescue from oblivion the appearance of his subjects. Rockmore, like Catlin, frequently painted several pictures a day. His paintings were not only records of the model's appearance but also a tribute to the artist's perception. Often an individual painting in either series thrusts forward with that overpowering quality called "presence," and even those which are less dynamic show the compassion of the creative mind. Both artists worked from live models, using free, quick, spontaneous layins. The additional detail and development of a painting were confined to the commitment undertaken by the first strokes. Rockmore, like Catlin, is a pure artist of considerable sensitivity.

Those who feel that Rockmore subjugated his talent to documentation should realize the sacrifice was justified. The combination of skill and dedication which both he and Catlin exercised resulted in these fantastic collections. It is noteworthy that in each case the artist chose to remain objective and resisted the "cheaply bought" success of painting flattering pictures, glamorizing their subjects as folk heroes. It is easier to appreciate the scope and grandeur of the Catlin project when one sees many of the paintings together. It is similarly true that the total impact of the Rockmore paintings is best felt when viewing a large part of the collection. Visitors drawn to Preservation Hall by the music often unexpectedly discover the presence of the paintings and are profoundly moved.

This series has evoked widespread admiration, although occasionally a connoisseur observes that in some instances the personality of the model may have been modified to restate the artist's mystically profound credo. Rockmore's major creative contribution is in the realm of fantasy. The scope of his career transcends the Preservation Hall portraits, although these have a very special place. The introspective mastery which enabled him to execute these remarkable likenesses is evidenced in all of Rockmore's works, as is his chosen theme: *Time is running out for us all*.

Rockmore and Chicken Henry in front of the Hall

THE PROPRIETORS

Bill Russell

Allan P. Jaffe, impresario and sometime tuba player, comes from a musical family. His grandfather played French horn for a Russian Imperial Army band, and his father played a mandolin and taught in the Philadelphia Settlement Music School that later became part of the famed Curtis Institute.

Allan was born in Pottsville, Pennsylvania, in 1935. At age five he started playing piano, and by twelve he was taking cornet lessons. In junior high school he switched to tuba because it was bigger. In high school he made the All-State Band and won a scholarship to Valley Forge Military Academy. His schedule there included two parades daily, plus rehearsals and concert tours. He attended the University of Pennsylvania and graduated from the Wharton School of Finance. After graduation he joined the army and was stationed at Fort Polk, Louisiana, a happy circumstance which led to his first direct exposure to New Orleans jazz.

Sandra Smolen Jaffe was born March 10, 1938, in Philadelphia. Her mother, once a professional pianist, saw to it that she was given piano lessons from the age of six. However, she had no desire to become a

professional musician, and instead studied English and journalism at
Harcum Junior College and the University of Pennsylvania.

   While Allan was in college, he heard a Louis Armstrong concert at
the Philadelphia Academy of Music which sparked his interest in
New Orleans jazz. He started to buy records by Armstrong, Bunk Johnson,
and George Lewis, and he and Sandy listened to them by the hour.
When they were married in 1960, following Allan's army hitch, they
decided to move to New Orleans. They took jobs and started looking for
live music. One night in the spring of 1961 they chanced upon some
members of the Eureka Brass Band on their way to a concert at
the Cabildo. This was the first real New Orleans group they had heard
in person, and they followed the band up St. Peter Street to Borenstein's
Gallery, where there was more informal music making. After that came
Sunday afternoon sessions at the gallery, where they heard such musicians
as George Lewis, Punch Miller, Kid Thomas, and Creole George
Guesnon.

In September, 1961, the Jaffes were asked to take over the operation of Preservation Hall and immediately accepted. They began tackling the dozens of tasks that needed doing, such as getting the old upright piano reconditioned, subduing the lighting, and arranging for seating. At last the sign, fashioned out of battered musical instrument cases, was hung, and its outline became the trademark of the Hall.

From the beginning, the Jaffes depended on word of mouth rather than advertising to publicize the Hall. Soon photographers and writers from publications everywhere found the saga of the Hall worth telling. Movie sequences and network television shows filmed there added to its growing reputation.

Allan did not give up his tuba, but began to listen to the New Orleans horn men, among them Wilbert Tillman who played at the Hall with John Casimir's band. He learned the New Orleans style by coaching from Sweet Emma, Punch Miller, and Guesnon. He absorbed the repertoire and became one of the best brass band parade sousaphonists in town. He frequently sits in with bands playing at the Hall. Allan now spends considerable time on the road, managing tours that have taken the musicians to all parts of the country, as well as to Europe and Japan.

Sandy's chores at the Hall are many and varied. During performances she can usually be found holding the antique wicker basket which serves as the "kitty." Prior to starting time, she is busy arranging seats and floor cushions, opening the shutters, and sweeping out the puddles that accumulate from afternoon rains in the carriageway. Before that, there are letters and notes to write and a dozen matters to attend to, including, occasionally, brewing coffee for George Lewis and Cie Frazier, cooling water for Punch Miller's medicine, and warming Sweet Emma's soup. All in all, it is a busy but satisfying life for both of the Jaffes.

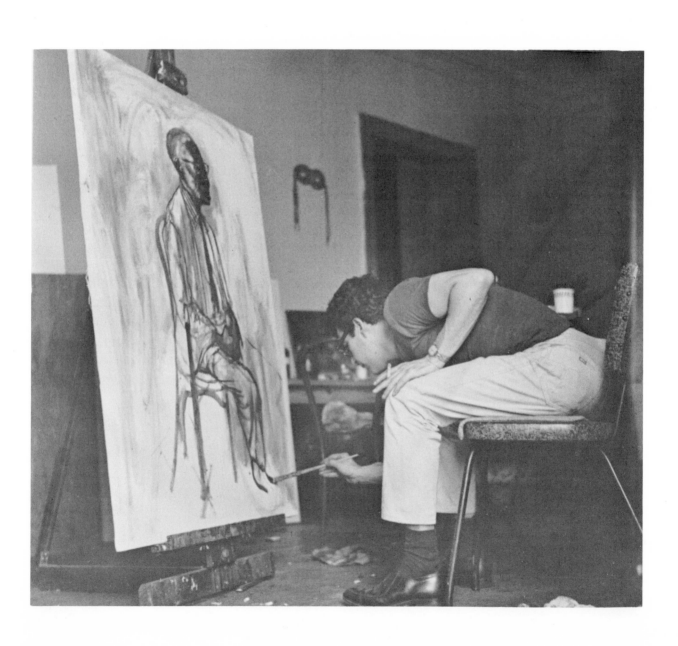

ROCKMORE
on the Preservation Hall Portraits

A Conversation with Bill Russell

The Preservation Hall series of paintings consists of two types, polymers and oils. The oils are the major works in the series. The polymers, usually small in size, can be thought of as studies for the oils because most of them were executed in the Hall during actual performances. There is also a small section of collages, including one of Joe James in which his vest (paper from an old New Orleans album) is glued on.

The approach had not been entirely formulated prior to the time I began this series of paintings. But as I got into the subject, and as the basic theme evolved, the sense of Past, the sense of powerful, lonely configuration, and the idea of a sort of simple strength started coming through. The opportunity to depict these individuals—literally *living legends*—was also a challenge. The problem for me as a painter was to bring a musical past visually into contemporaneous terms. I had to recapture a past that was indeed magical as long as it was the present.

In these paintings I attempted to recognize the funereal feeling which I think permeates New Orleans creativity. This creativity has largely been limited to jazz, probably the only original art form which has evolved in America. My paintings have come under some criticism for having a macabre or an overly sad feeling at times, but I think the subject matter itself is overly sad. It *is* the past. The somberness of these paintings is partially due to the dignity of the musicians. Dignity is not humor. It has humor in it, but it is not funny. For example, Egyptian sculpture does not make you laugh, and it is in this sense that the paintings are sad, if they are successful. If I failed to retain an element of dignity in certain paintings, I think in most cases at least I have not turned to caricature.

Some of the men, like Frank Amacker or Slow Drag, are essentially humorous in their sadness. However, in most cases a feeling of somberness comes through, even in Percy Humphrey, to whose portraits I tried to impart a quality of hunched-over power. A man like Babe Stovall exudes a plaintive quality of suffering and loneliness. Many of the men do not have this quality. Jim Robinson doesn't have it at all. He's like a big child. Visually, Jim Robinson has the structure of a physical giant, and when he sits down he seems almost monolithic. An artist can't paint a humorous painting of this, and if he paints a charming one he misses the point. He has to choose very carefully between the superficialities and the basics. And the basics are the somberness, the hieratic dignity of *most* of the men, the lack of intellectuality and yet the intelligence. So we have subject matter that is fundamentally human, and yet also specific—they're all musicians.

I think that the free and original structured form of pure New Orleans jazz was the meat of the genuine creative explosion. The classic form of jazz is very similar in some ways to Bach in that you have some fugal style—a little counterpoint here and there. In terms of my own background, I think that my study of the violin as a child at Juilliard (and later of the classic guitar) has tended to make me more conscious of a "Bach" approach to music—basically simple forms that play against each other, although this is a tremendous oversimplification. Early jazz is the only form of jazz that uses this approach. I'm aware that some later men in our own era claim to have done this, but I find their music much more arbitrary and meandering compared to the very simple, strict, early form of jazz. And the early form is what appeals to me. I don't feel that the jazz that followed it is as good. I don't feel that it is as sound, solid, or revolutionary. The music wasn't meant to be *all* improvisation. It has a definite and restricted form at its best.

The meat of any movement lasts only a few years. Cubism, the most important movement in this century in painting, lasted, in its truly revolutionary phase, only a few years. Its dates—that is, the creative dates— are roughly from 1907 to 1914. The meat of the four or five basic forms in Cubist thinking happened within a very few years, and I think the same is true of the much simpler fundamental forms of jazz. I feel the later forms have lost a kind of pioneer feeling, as has almost everything else in our lives. I feel that the early jazz that I respond to most relates to my own background in music, even though my training had nothing to do with jazz. I think that's the explanation of why I felt a kinship to the subject matter of the New Orleans series.

I started violin at three and a half and had Ruggiero Ricci's half-size violin. I studied music to the exclusion of normal schooling for several years, but this was interrupted by illness. I began to paint when I was about seven, and the first things I did were little pencil drawings of my left hand. Although my parents were artists, they had more to do with pushing me into music than painting, and when I started to paint completely on my own I was far away from home at a school in Vermont. I flunked almost all of my courses because I worked in the art studio eight hours a day. So school for me was a complete and total farce and consisted of only two subjects, painting and reading—a tremendous amount of reading because vocabulary is essential to developing your mind. If you can't work with words then you're not going to be able to think out the things you want to think out. And this has to do with restriction of means and technique in painting, music, literature, etc.—the use of words as a tool, the same as any other tool, visually or musically.

As a painter I was largely self-taught, and because of that I made many mistakes. When you teach yourself in the field of painting or etching, for example, you make so many technical and physical blunders. You can burn your hand in acid as I did, and so on. You literally don't know not to put your hand into an acid bath, but on the other hand, by not studying with instructors, you do avoid the shortcuts. You have to go around the long way and you pick up a tremendous amount of other knowledge that might be useful.

In my early work the subject matter was essentially the same as it is now. At twenty-three, for example, I was doing a family portrait, which is a very somber painting of four people separated. The word "separation" here is important because that is pretty much what the jazz figures are. They are isolated within four sides of a two-dimensional field, as they are pretty much in their lives. We can touch each other, and talk, and communicate, but basically we all are alone in life, and I think that somehow this sense of isolation as a basic concept runs through and permeates my work. Even the earliest things that I did in Mexico in 1946 and 1948 dealt with separation of one from another.

The first seven or eight years of my development in painting techniques consisted of drawing, etching, and lithography, and then very *tight* oil techniques which lasted for several years, until I was about twenty-six or twenty-seven years old, at which point I took up tempera as a discipline. Egg tempera is a discipline, because you use the yolk of an egg, and you have to work very slowly and prepare your paint fresh every morning. This physical limitation forces you to paint more slowly and therefore to think differently from the way you usually think. Even though I may have painted slowly and with great detail in an oil such as *The Artist in Coney Island*, for example, which was done when I was twenty-nine, the painting itself didn't take very long because the decisions were usually made before the actual pigment was put down.

Larry Borenstein's commission on the Preservation Hall series of musicians was a jolt to most of the work habits I'd had, because they generally had to be done in one sitting. I think this had a very good effect, at least for a while, on my work. I think that when an artist is forced to deal with a new set of circumstances, he either sinks or swims, and I think that in swimming rather vigorously I learned, literally, new techniques, at a relatively late stage—I was thirty-four when I started the series. The jazz series itself pretty much encapsulates my entire career. The first polymers were mixtures of pen and ink drawings and painting, and were tremendously detailed, because of my insecurity in the medium. These were the forerunners of the oils (some 40 x 60 inches or, in a few cases, even larger) done in one sitting, sometimes with a furious impasto. Being forced to work without the technique that I spent so many years devising was, I think, good for me. I think it also helped me to put down spontaneously a very strong impression of each musician as he sat in the studio. I believe I could have gotten bogged down from the actual idea of the series of paintings had I used a slower technique. I feel strongly that *all* intrinsic or genuine developments in an artist are essentially *against* the grain—if the creator only repeats what he has done he naturally will go only so far.

The studio above Preservation Hall had a great deal of mood and atmosphere that was conducive to the series. I got along particularly well with George Lewis. He is a febrile, nervous, sensitive-looking man, and a delightful subject. A very successful grisaille portrait of him was sold to a London collector. It was one of the first times that I ever did a pure drawing on a large canvas with almost no pigment in it. And this was *George*, very much. The clarinet was the thickest and strongest part of the whole painting, *physically*. George barely hangs on to the thing, visually speaking. He's like a little, delicate, long-legged spider, and a small one at that, somehow producing an element of power when he plays. I tried to paint him that way. And I painted him four or five times.

The large Israel Gorman portrait was one of the major oils. It was a semi-grisaille, differing from the George Lewis in that, perhaps influenced by my old egg tempera technique, I used a transparent wash to create a sort of glaze over a drawing. This painting was started down in the Jaffe's patio with about a dozen people around, then finished upstairs in the studio with Jules Cahn taking a movie—and with several other things going on. The painting definitely reflects the crowded room and the feeling of activity around the subject.

I think that Israel Gorman during that sitting came through to me as a lonely little man clutching an instrument as a security symbol. Partially because he wasn't playing it during the time he was posing, the clarinet was almost a useless object in his hands, and yet at the same time it was the thing he knew best. I saw him as a trembling sort of creature, capable of anger and yet at the same time repressed. The sense of quietude in the little figure is expressed better in another Gorman painting in which there is a huge slab of impasto (brilliant cadmium red) —a very interesting painting in which the slab of red more or less crushes the figure. The figure is quite small in a large canvas, precisely the opposite of the usual jazz painting in which the object, that is the figure, is large.

Louis Nelson is physically a handsome man—striking high cheekbones and the flowing quality of his physical structure made him a magnificent model and produced some of the best paintings. Joe Watkins is another marvelous model, but I only painted him one time. Punch Miller I painted several times and Chicken Henry at least twenty times. The relationship with Chicken Henry was a strange one, a personal relationship

more than just a purely visual one. Punch is a marvelous guy to paint because the planes on his face are so obvious. You can almost hang onto them physically to save your life, and I think that had a lot to do with the success of the various Punch Miller paintings. I think the Johnny Wiggs portrait, which leaves large areas of the canvas untouched, is one of the finest in the whole series. It is a small painting but one of the most sensitive and delicate.

At this point I'd like to mention the relationship of the figures to various shaped instruments. I think this is a fascinating element, because the fact is that visually the instruments end up *belonging* to those who play them. By this I mean that Israel Gorman could not possibly hold a trombone. George Lewis would be crushed to death by one. On the other hand the thought of Jim Robinson or Louis Nelson playing a piccolo or a clarinet is ludicrous. The idea of Joe Watkins even being away from his drums is like that of a newlywed being away from his wife. As a *visual idea* this is very important. I think that some of that feeling, of the men belonging to their trade, is very strong in the series. I tried to get this feeling into the entire group of paintings, and, in general, I think it came through—men isolated in time, belonging to a *trade*.

The choice of canvas size is always an emotional one, and I always make sure I have a large selection. If a man comes in and he feels "squat" to me I get a big square one. If he's a tiny figure I might take a large canvas and place him in the corner of it. Andrew Morgan would tend to fill out a space, whereas a man like George Lewis would not, but you can actually approach both men in the same way if you wish, and it produces a different kind of painting. The choice of size is like the choice of color, which tends to be not so much conscious chromaticism as sudden emotional impulse for, say, a blue in a certain area—you just *feel blue* in that area. It's not so much that you know intellectually that blue and red are going to work well in that area. Although size generally is an emotional thing, there's always a rationalization. Louis Nelson has a tendency, for example, to spread his legs very wide when he's sitting down, his trombone at an angle, and as a result several paintings of him are almost square—simply to accommodate the position into which he naturally fell. I tried to work with the subject on a visual and a rather structural plane, and to avoid constriction wherever possible.

Of course, out of all of the musicians, close to a hundred of them, I guess, some were magnificent subjects and others presented real difficulties. One man I didn't relate to, or particularly like as a person, was one of the great subjects because he's like a huge Egyptian sculpture, literally. He affects me exactly the same way; the planes on his head, and the strange shaped skull and so on, are built for a painter. It means he practically paints the picture; all I have to do is just let the lines go where they want to go. But there aren't too many like that.

I believe that my paintings reproduce well in black and white. Unless color reproduction is absolutely first-rate, and therefore incredibly expensive, it is not worth using because of its inaccuracies. It is harder for black and white reproduction to be inaccurate because it is a simpler process. My work usually reproduces well in black and white because of the design factor. Contrast is a very strong element in my painting. It is my nature as a painter to design masses with separation of lines, not as an outline but separation of one mass from another with a line—

the mass in between the lines, as it were. This contrast of one area against another, light and dark, tends to reproduce very strongly in black and white. Cezanne doesn't reproduce well in black and white because he literally is a chromatic painter. Seurat is a chromatic painter in terms of pointellism, but the pointellist areas are broken up into beautifully articulated design and as a result his work reproduces well in black and white. My work is even more specifically designed and isolated, one area against another, with little loss in reproduction without color. The only power color has is perhaps similar to timbre in music. There is an emotional appeal to color—a psychological impact. It has no other importance to *me* in painting. I think the important things are drawing, how you articulate an area, and how you design the masses. Those are the things that make a painting last after color has perhaps yellowed with time. Design can't yellow with time. Therefore, I think it is a stronger element in painting.

It's difficult to talk about jazz without getting into very subjective stuff like the effect of the Hall personally on me. You know I'd tend to be less critical there than I would if I heard the music on records. I mean, how can you look into DeDe Pierce's face, which is the blind-trumpeter-of-all-time face, and be objective? I feel that in this country there's a tremendous lack of appreciation for the miracle that happened around the turn of the century in New Orleans. I'm absolutely convinced that this was America's musical renaissance. Sociologically, I cannot analyze the reasons for America's relative inability to deal with larger classic forms on a first-rate level, but it is fairly obvious that we have failed in our attempt to equal Beethoven, Mozart, Schubert, and so on. We've had two centuries to at least attempt it. It's like saying women have not had a chance. Well, they've had at least three centuries of more leisure than the breadwinner. Structurally, women generally may be more intelligent. In my experience they are—more so than most men, whom I often find rather stupid. But they have too many glands to cope with. They cannot sit in a room for thirty-five years like Cezanne and develop a concept in absolute isolation. That's why they're not Shakespeares and that's why they're not Beethovens or Rembrandts. They may hit the secondary level perhaps, like Elizabeth Barrett Browning and Mme. Curie, but they don't get into that first level because they can't have first level isolation and still remain a woman. It's not possible for them.

I don't know if this series of paintings is going to be the best series I'll ever do, but I think some of them will be among the strongest. For example, I think the Punch Miller (with the hand on his leg—a 40 x 50 done in about an hour and a half, with red and green in the background) is particularly strong, direct, and simple. It's a very fine painting in my estimation—and I dislike much of my work. But I think I produced some good ones. I believe that the historical element of the paintings is relatively unimportant—after all, photography can record. But I think that the communal attitude in which these paintings came about— movies being taken by Jules Cahn, Tom Sancton coming around to the studio—was inspiratory in several ways, and I think that's important. And I think this feeling got into some of the paintings.

I enjoy hanging around and listening to the bands at the Hall, even though it's sad. It's important to have memories, and you don't have a chance to see the memories walking around very often, so maybe that's what it means to me personally. And at least it reminds me of a really great period.

THE

PORTRAITS

ADAMS, DOLLY (MARIE DOUROUX)—piano

b. January 11, 1904, New Orleans

Dolly Adams is the daughter of a sister of Manuel Manetta. Her mother played piano, violin, and trumpet; and her father, Louis Douroux, was a trumpeter with the Excelsior Brass Band. He also played occasionally with other brass bands and orchestras.

Dolly began playing the piano when she was about seven years old. Later she went to St. Mary's Academy, where she learned scales and fingering. By the time she was nine she was accompanying her brother, who played the violin. At thirteen she began playing the piano occasionally with Manuel Manetta, and during this time she played with Louis Armstrong, Kid Ory, Joe Oliver, Alex Bigard, and other greats. When she was in her twenties, she led her own band at the Othello Theater. Later she became the pianist with Peter Bocage and played spot jobs with Luis "Papa" Tio, Lorenzo Tio, Jr., and Alphonse Picou. She left Bocage's band when she was married, about 1922, and did not play in bands for the fifteen years during which she raised her family.

In 1937 Dolly started again with her brothers Lawrence and Irving Douroux, and she played with them until Irving's death. She then organized a trio with two of her sons, Justin and Gerald, and enlarged it to a quartet when Placide, her other son, was discharged from the Army. After the war the Adams family played occasionally as a unit, but for the most part the individual members found jobs with other groups.

Since 1961 most of Dolly's playing has been at Preservation Hall as leader of her own group, as well as with such bands as those of Punch Miller, George Lewis, Captain John Handy, and "Creole George" Guesnon. In 1966 she suffered a slight stroke and temporarily retired, but she has since recovered and has resumed her career.

Dolly Adams is one of the finest exponents of pure New Orleans style jazz piano, yet up to the present time she has not been recorded.

AMACKER, FRANK—guitar, piano

b. March 22, 1890, New Orleans

Frank Amacker, nicknamed "Dude," comes to Preservation Hall as often as he can to listen to the music and reminisce with tourists, musicians, and historians about the old days in "Storyville." Occasionally he will break into song in a falsetto or be invited onto the stand to play a number. He has a following of faithful admirers, who enjoy his anecdotes and his warm sense of humor. For a period he was intermission pianist at Preservation Hall, until this practice was discontinued.

In 1966 Dude was recorded at the Hall on a solo LP by Pearl Records. In the fifties he was recorded by Folkways on a track featuring a jazz rendition of "Traumerei," but his great skill is as a solo ragtime pianist. Occasionally, after a concert, he holds court at the piano for a small, select audience.

An impeccable dresser, Dude is meticulous in every detail of his appearance and is in many ways the embodiment of the spirit of jazz. He was the only musician in his family and learned to play the guitar when he was about ten years old. By the time he was fifteen he had had some piano lessons at Southern University under Professor William Nickerson, and when he was sixteen he was playing in bands in the District.

His first job was at the 101 Ranch on Franklin Street, where musicians included Jimmy Palao, George Baquet, Ernest Trepagnier, and Billy Marrero. He also played with the Celestin band, and before long he was a full-fledged "professor," playing solo piano in the parlors of such well-known Basin Street houses as Countess Willie Piazza's, Gypsy Shaffer's on Robertson Street, and Eloise Blankenstein's.

After the District closed, Frank found his way to the West Coast and played guitar and piano in Los Angeles. Returning to New Orleans, he played spot jobs as a featured soloist with various bands.

ANDERSON, ANDREW—trumpet

b. August 10, 1905, Mandeville, La.

Andy Anderson's father, George Anderson, was a bass player who played with Bunk Johnson in Mandeville about 1915–18. Andrew's brother bought him a cornet from an old trumpet player, who wrote the scales down for Andy. After Andy had been playing for about a year, he took a correspondence course from the American School of Music.

His first professional job was in 1925–26 with Willie Foster's band at Buck Humphrey's place on the levee. Then in 1927 Andy organized the Pelican Silvertone Band. He also played at the Alamo dance hall and the Lavida taxi dance hall with Paul Barnes and Jim Robinson. Later he worked at the Entertainers' Club, at Franklin and Iberville streets, a favorite hangout for musicians and the popular after-hours spot in the District. In the early thirties he was at the Budweiser taxi dance hall and later with A. J. Piron's band on the steamers *J.S.* and *President.* From 1934 to 1940 he played with Papa Celestin's Tuxedo Band, and in the fifties was with Paul Barbarin on two "Wide, Wide World" telecasts. He recorded with George Lewis for Verve while on a West Coast trip in 1959, and later that year he recorded with the Young Tuxedo Brass Band on the Atlantic release "Jazz Begins." In these bands he played first trumpet. Andy currently leads the Pelican State Band.

He has appeared at Preservation Hall with John Casimir's Young Tuxedo Band, which included Bill Matthews, Alfred Williams, Wilbert Tillman, and Charlie Hamilton. After Casimir's death, Wilbert Tillman became leader and Andrew Morgan replaced Casimir. After Alfred Williams' death, Joe Watkins replaced him on drums, and after Bill Matthews' death, Albert Warner replaced him on trombone. Shortly thereafter, Wilbert Tillman suffered a stroke, and the band as such broke up. Andy's appearances at the Hall lately have been few.

BARKER, DANNY—banjo, guitar

b. January 13, 1909, New Orleans

Danny Barker comes from a musical family. His grandfather was Isidore Barbarin, and his great-uncle was Louis Arthidore, who played with the Onward Brass Band before the Spanish-American War.

Danny started playing banjo in 1925. He took lessons from George Augustin and watched and listened to the old master banjoists, such as John Marrero, Caffrey Darensburg, Johnny St. Cyr, and Emanuel Sayles. He had his first job at sixteen with Willie Pajeaud's Jazz Band at the Alamo dance hall on Canal and Burgundy streets.

He played occasionally with other bands, including those of Lee Collins, Buddy Petit, Kid Rena, and David Jones, until 1930 when he went to New York and began playing with Lucky Millinder. He stayed on there and was part of the New York jazz scene, except for return visits, until 1965 when he came back to New Orleans. In New York he played with Baron Lee, Benny Carter, Fess Williams, and, on two occasions, he led bands at Jimmy Ryan's club. He also worked with Cab Calloway for about ten years and toured extensively.

Since Danny's return to New Orleans, he has appeared at Preservation Hall occasionally, playing with Johnny Wiggs' band and with Percy Humphrey. He cannot, however, properly be called a Preservation Hall musician because his style, which was developed outside of New Orleans, frequently does not fit in with that of traditional bands. He is presently working on a book of his jazz memoirs, which covers his forty-year career. The September, 1965, *Evergreen Review* published excerpts from this work.

Danny has recorded with many big names, such as Louis Armstrong, Ethel Waters, Billie Holiday, Charlie Parker, Jonah Jones, Wingy Manone, Wild Bill Davison, and Tony Parenti. Danny's wife, Blue Lu Barker, sings blues and recorded for Decca in the mid-thirties. Much of her material was composed and arranged by Danny.

BARNES, EMILE—clarinet

b. February 18, 1892, New Orleans

One of a famous New Orleans musical family, Emile Barnes, along with his brother Paul, claims kinship with the Marreros, the Fraziers, and the Smiths. His first instrument was a toy fife. Later he had a flute. In his teens he ran around with Sidney Bechet, and together they listened to Alphonse Picou and Big Eye Louis Nelson. They followed parades, went to dance halls, and did everything they could to acquaint themselves with the style of their idols.

His first clarinet was given to him by Bunk Johnson, who also gave him some help in learning to play, but he actually studied with Lorenzo Tio, Sr., Alphonse Picou, and George Baquet. At eighteen he formed his own dance band called the Boys in Blue, and their first job was at Delacroix Island. In 1913 he played with Edward Clem and later with Vic and Oak Gaspard. After World War I he played with Johnny Brown's band and still later with Chris Kelly, with whom he was associated until Kelly's death in 1927. Emile has also played with Kid Howard in the house orchestra at the Palace Theater, with Lawrence Toca at the Harmony Inn, with Billie and DeDe Pierce playing weekends at Luthjen's dance hall, and with the Superior and Olympic Brass Bands. Emile was recorded on American Music in 1951, and in 1961 he was recorded with the Kid Thomas Algiers Stompers on Riverside. He was also recorded on Icon.

During the early days of Preservation Hall, Emile Barnes was heard frequently both as leader of his own group and with Billie and DeDe Pierce or with Charlie Love. However, by 1963, feeling no longer able to take on a four-hour job, he stopped playing.

He is still keenly interested in music and frequently sets up informal sessions on Sunday afternoons in his backyard. He supports himself by running a candy store across the street from a school in the Ninth Ward, where he has lived most of his life. Often, when he is not busy, he sits out on his front steps in the sun playing to himself.

MELEY BARNES

NO. 50

'63

Rockmore

April 14

BARNES, PAUL D. ("POLO")—clarinet

b. November 22, 1902, New Orleans

When Paul Barnes was six, his older brother Emile gave him his first instrument, a toy fife. Ten years later he took piano lessons at St. Paul's Lutheran College. When he was eighteen he went to a circus and saw Jazzbo Curry playing a tenor sax, which gave him an interest in the instrument, but on the advice of his cousin John Marrero he purchased an alto sax instead.

His first professional job was in September of 1919. Soon he formed his own group, the Original Diamond Jazz Band, which included Josiah Frazier on drums, George Washington on trombone, Eddie Marrero on bass, Lawrence Marrero on banjo, and Bush Hall on trumpet. In 1922 the band changed its name to the Young Tuxedo Orchestra. Later Paul joined Kid Rena's band. In 1923 he joined the Maple Leaf Orchestra and then the Original Tuxedo Orchestra at Tranchina's. The Original Tuxedo Orchestra split up, but Paul stayed with Papa Celestin until 1927, when he joined King Oliver on tour. In 1928 he joined Jelly Roll Morton's Red Hot Peppers, which recorded for Victor in 1929, and then he rejoined King Oliver in 1931. In 1932 he formed a band at Lake Charles, which included Nellie Lutcher on piano, DeDe Pierce on trumpet, and Chester Zardis on bass. In 1934 he rejoined King Oliver on tour, and in 1935 he returned to New Orleans, where he worked with Willie Pajeaud at the Budweiser dance hall. In 1936 he joined Kid Howard at the Lavida taxi dance hall, where he stayed through 1939. During the war he was in the Navy Band and went to the Navy Music School in Washington, D.C., attaining the rank of Musician First Class. After the war he rejoined Celestin's Tuxedo Orchestra. He moved to Los Angeles in 1951, and in 1958 he played for the Southern California Hot Jazz Society with Johnny St. Cyr, Alton Purnell, and others.

Back in New Orleans in 1960, he joined Paul Barbarin's band. He has recorded with Charlie Love, the Kid Thomas band, the Eureka Brass Band, and with his own group. In 1961–62 and in 1963 he played at Disneyland with Johnny St. Cyr and Kid Ory. He returned to New Orleans in 1964 and appears frequently at Preservation Hall, playing most often with Billie and DeDe Pierce.

BARRETT, EMMA ("SWEET EMMA THE BELL GAL")—piano

b. March 25, 189?, New Orleans

Emma Barrett says that a woman who will tell her age will tell anything. Emma's career dates back at least to 1923, when she played with Celestin and Ridgley in the Original Tuxedo Orchestra. In 1925, when Celestin left Ridgley, and each formed his own Tuxedo Orchestra, Emma remained with Ridgley, an association which lasted until 1936. During this period Emma often worked under John Robichaux, A. J. Piron, and Sidney Desvigne.

Photographs taken of Emma in the twenties show a beautiful girl. Her trademark is a pair of red garters with bells attached, which she manages to jingle furiously while she plays. Emma does not read music, but she has the ability to follow anything after hearing it once. She also transposes effortlessly. New Orleans musicians refer to this as "cross chording"; it is often necessary for a pianist to do this because New Orleans pianos are rarely in tune and almost never on pitch. As a result, the "blowing instruments" have trouble getting right with the piano, and, unless the pianist can cross chord, the whole band is out of tune. This happens more often than anyone likes to admit and is one reason why the banjo is popular with New Orleans bands.

Emma will not fly even if she has to pass up a lucrative job. In 1964, when her band went to Disneyland for a television appearance, she left two days early in order to go by train, although the rest of the band flew. The same kind of arrangements were necessary for her October, 1964, appearance at the Tyrone Guthrie Theater in Minneapolis.

Emma has been recorded as leader of her own group on Southland, Riverside, and on the Preservation Hall label. She appeared at Preservation Hall frequently as leader of her own group and as pianist for other groups until she suffered a slight stroke in 1967. She made a triumphant reappearance in March, 1968, in the Grand Ballroom of the Royal Orleans Hotel to play for the Heart Fund Jazz Band Jamboree. Since then she has appeared occasionally at Preservation Hall.

BIGARD, ALEX—drums

b. September 25, 1898, New Orleans

Alex Bigard has been a professional musician most of his life. He and his brothers Barney and Sidney had a kid trio. After a couple of years of instruction from Louis Cottrell, Sr., Alex got replacement jobs with the best bands, working with Manuel Perez and Alphonse Picou in the famous Maple Leaf Orchestra, and occasionally replacing his teacher with the Piron orchestra.

His first regular gig was at Tom Anderson's carbaret, but he soon graduated to Kid Shots Madison's band. In the twenties he joined Sidney Desvigne's orchestra in which his uncle Emile Bigard played violin. This was one of the favorite bands of Beansie Fauria, the leading musical promoter of the period, and it appeared frequently at the Astoria and at the San Jacinto Club.

John Robichaux hired Alex for the pit band at the old Lyric Theater in the mid-twenties, and although the job ended when the Lyric burned down, Alex stayed with the band until Robichaux died in 1939. He then joined the band at the Black and Tan cabaret. When this club closed, he went to the Brown Derby with Kid Rena and later to the Cadillac Club. In the fifties his own group, the Mighty Four, played weekends at the Melody Inn. In 1956 they moved to the Harmony Inn, another downtown dance hall, but before long the owners switched to a western music policy. At that time jazz jobs in New Orleans were at their lowest ebb. Alex had occasional jobs but nothing regular until 1960, when he came to one of the art gallery sessions with Harold Dejan. From then on, Alex played frequently with various groups, most often with Billie and DeDe Pierce and George Guesnon, until his retirement in 1967.

Alex recorded with Kid Clayton's band in 1951 on Folkways, with Punch Miller's band in 1960 on Icon, and with Kid Sheik in 1961 on Mono.

BOCAGE, PETER—trumpet, violin, trombone, banjo, xylophone

b. July 31, 1887, Algiers, La.
d. December 3, 1967, New Orleans

Peter Bocage is the best known member of a musical family. His career dates back to 1906 when he played violin with Tom Albert's band. From about 1908 to 1910 he was violinist and leader of the Superior Orchestra with Bunk Johnson and Big Eye Louis Nelson. For several years he played violin in various District joints such as the Tuxedo dance hall, Tom Anderson's and the "Big 25."

By 1918 Bocage had become proficient on the cornet and played a season with Fate Marable on the S.S.*Capitol*. Then for several years he was associated with A. J. Piron, a violinist and music publisher who had a popular society orchestra with such prominent musicians as Lorenzo Tio, Jr., Steve Lewis, John Lindsay, and Louis Cottrell. Peter usually played cornet with Piron but at times played trombone or another instrument. The group traveled to New York in 1924–25 and was recorded by three leading companies. Peter also arranged music for the Piron band and composed several numbers, some of which, including "Bouncing Around" and the hit "Mamma's Gone, Goodbye," were recorded by Piron. In the late twenties Piron's orchestra disbanded and Peter helped reorganize it as the Creole Serenaders, which had a popular following for many years. In the mid-forties Bocage played with Big Eye Louis' band on weekends at Luthjen's dance hall, and in 1945 he spent a month in Boston, where he was reunited with Sidney Bechet at a Savoy Café engagement.

Peter was also long active in brass band parades. He took over the leadership of the pioneer Excelsior Brass Band after the death of George Moret, and in 1960 he became a regular member of the Eureka Brass Band, with which he paraded until a few months before his death.

Bocage recorded with the Zenith Brass Band in 1946, with the Creole Serenaders in 1961 on the Riverside "Living Legends" series, and with the Eureka Brass Band in 1962 on Atlantic.

Peter appeared at Preservation Hall frequently with his Creole Serenaders. Whenever the group played his arrangement of Piron's old theme song "Purple Rose of Cairo," he always took choruses on violin as well as trumpet to make this beautiful number a memorable example of New Orleans music.

BUTLER, JOSEPH ("TWAT")—bass

b. December 25, 1907, Algiers, La.

Joseph Butler's first instrument was a homemade one-string bass. As a boy he and Red Allen shared an early interest in jazz. They followed parades together, and occasionally Twat would "keep time" for Red while Red was practicing. Except for a few lessons with Pinchback Touro, Twat taught himself to play the bass.

His first job was on a three-day trip to Grand Isle with Raymond Brown's band, which included Sammy Penn. In his early twenties Twat had his first steady job with Nolan Williams, a drummer from Houma. For thirty-five years now he has been more or less regularly associated with Kid Thomas Valentine, though in his early days he played with such leaders as A. J. Piron, Sidney Desvigne, Fats Pichon, and Papa Celestin.

There was a period in which Twat "bummed" around the District, and his nickname harks back to those days. In the early days of Preservation Hall, Sandy Jaffe always called him "Twat" when introducing the band. It was almost a year before she learned of its slang context. Since then he has been called "Joseph Butler" around Preservation Hall but probably nowhere else. At the Hall he works with the Kid Thomas band and occasionally with Sweet Emma. He has been recorded with Kid Thomas on Riverside and Icon and with Billie and DeDe Pierce on Mono.

His "Big Lunch Blues," numbered from one to twenty, is a series of soliloquies which recount his Depression experiences. Some are as long as ten or twelve minutes, and none are less than five. They tell of economical and emotional problems which Twat surmounts through sheer fortitude and end on a happy note which sums up his philosophy:

> "Some day, some day
> Everything will be okay
> It may be tomorrow
> Or it may be the first of May."

CAGNOLATTI, ERNIE—trumpet

b. April 2, 1911, Madisonville, La.

As a boy of five or six, Ernie Cagnolatti listened to Bunk Johnson's band, in which Ernie's older brother Klebert was drummer, and it was Bunk's influence which led Ernie to choose the horn as his instrument. Ernie started on drums but switched to trumpet, partly, he says, because he was too small to lug a drum set around. For the most part, he was self-taught until he came to New Orleans at sixteen, where he had his first trumpet lessons with Arnold Metoyer.

Ernie's first professional job was about 1928, playing with Lionel Tapo. By 1932 he was good enough to be hired with Herbert Leary's big swing band, with which he played until 1940. He never lost touch, however, with the traditional New Orleans music and often played with George Lewis, Billie and DeDe Pierce, Albert Burbank, Kid Rena, Wooden Joe Nicholas, Paul Dominguez, Steve Lewis, Johnny St. Cyr, and Shots Madison. He also played with the Eureka and other brass bands led by "Old Man" Allen, Kid Howard, George Williams, and Harold Dejan. In 1951 he joined Paul Barbarin who played at the Gunga Din on Bourbon Street, the Mardi Gras Lounge, and the Famous Door. The band also made occasional trips, including an engagement at the Savoy Café in Boston. In 1953 Ernie joined Bill Matthews at the Paddock Lounge, an engagement which lasted until 1958.

Ernie recorded on Good Time Jazz with Paul Barbarin in 1956 and later with Bill Matthews' band. He also recorded on Riverside with Jim Robinson's New Orleans band, and in 1962 on Atlantic's "Jazz at Preservation Hall" series. His appearances at Preservation Hall are infrequent, but he does play occasionally with Jim Robinson, as a replacement for Percy Humphrey, or with George Lewis.

CLAYTON, JIMMY ("KID")—trumpet

b. March 2, 1902, Jasper County, Miss.
d. December 17, 1963, New Orleans

A specialist in the New Orleans blues style, Kid Clayton never learned much music, although he did study for a while with Professor Humphrey. Kid was a great favorite in the rough and tough neighborhood bands in the so-called "battlefield" area of uptown New Orleans. During the early twenties he joined Jack Carey's group, which played the rattiest jazz in New Orleans, and which is often credited with originating the band version of "Tiger Rag." For a while Kid toured with Dan Moody, making trips to rural Louisiana, the Mississippi Gulf Coast, and Memphis. Later he traveled with bands to Chicago, Ohio, and Texas. Back in New Orleans he played off and on at the Hummingbird Café with his own group, Kid Clayton and His Happy Pals.

During the depression he was in the WPA band, and old-timers like Wooden Joe Nicholas spoke of him as one of the most exciting horn men of that period. After the war he frequently took spot jobs and played as a replacement with other bands. There was also a period of engagements on the lake front, at Happy Landing, at Mamma Lou's, and occasionally at Little Woods camps.

Kid appeared on some tracks of the Folkways series "Music of New Orleans" and on a track of "Jazz at the Kitty Halls" issued by Arhoolie. He also led a group in recording an LP on Icon.

COLA, GEORGE ("KID SHEIK")—trumpet

b. September 15, 1908, New Orleans

George Cola's father and sisters always called him "Son," but to musicians and jazz enthusiasts he is known as "Sheik." As leader of his own band, the Storyville Ramblers, his theme song is "The Sheik of Araby," but he confides that the nickname was not won at music.

At twelve Sheik started to play the piano; for the most part, he taught himself. Later he took up the drums and finally the cornet. He took a few trumpet lessons from Wooden Joe Nicholas, and in 1925 he formed his own band. He was a childhood friend of Chris Kelly, and on a few occasions filled in for Kelly when he was sick. He also paraded with Willie Parker's Pacific Brass Band and Kid Rena's Brass Band.

Sheik's first professional dance job was at the Sorter's Inn near the slaughter house. The musicians were paid only $1.25 a night per man for six hours, but being paid at all was encouraging. He also played yard parties and an occasional dance, and from time to time he was second cornet with Buddy Petit and Chris Kelly. In 1934 he went to the U.S. Air Force Music School, and, when he returned to New Orleans in 1945, he formed another band. He also began playing as a replacement with the Eureka Brass Band, and in 1952 he replaced Eddie Richardson and has been with the band ever since.

Sheik is often heard at Preservation Hall, and in 1961 he took the first Preservation Hall jazz band tour to a two-week engagement at the Tudor Arms in Cleveland. He also made a tour to Washington, D.C. with the Eureka Brass Band for the First International Jazz Festival in 1962, toured England and Wales with Barry Martyn's band in 1963, and in 1967 took a band on a tour of Japan. He has been recorded twice with the Eureka Brass Band. He has also recorded with his Storyville Ramblers on Icon, and has had several British recording dates on Mono and other labels.

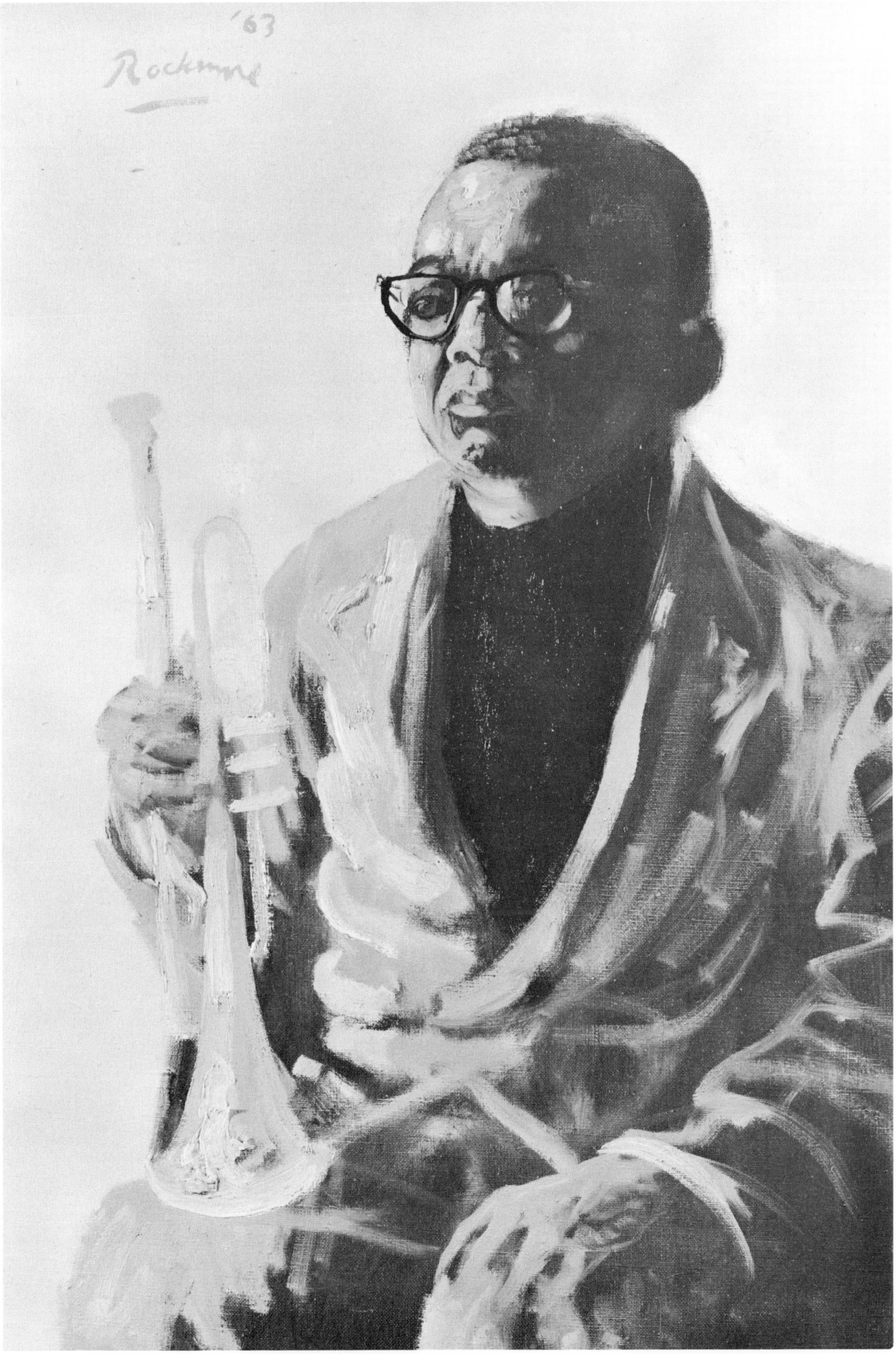
'63
Rockmore

COTTRELL, LOUIS, JR.—clarinet

b. March 7, 1911, New Orleans

Louis Cottrell's father was the famous drummer, Louis Cottrell, Sr., who played with A. J. Piron's orchestra. Louis, Jr., began playing the tenor saxophone and clarinet when he was a teen-ager. He was taught by clarinetist Lorenzo Tio, Jr.

By the early twenties Louis had established himself as a fine musician. He became a member of the Golden Rule Orchestra and also played in Lawrence Marrero's Young Tuxedo Orchestra. The mid-twenties saw him playing occasionally with A. J. Piron, and later with Bebe Ridgley's orchestra.

During the depression years, which were meager for nearly all New Orleans musicians, Louis played with Sidney Desvigne's orchestra. Then in 1940 he became a member of Paul Barbarin's band, and over the years he has played with most of the leading musicians in New Orleans.

In the thirties Louis recorded on tenor sax with the Don Albert band, but all of his later recordings featured him on clarinet. Riverside has recorded him with Peter Bocage's Creole Serenaders, with Jim Robinson's band, and as leader of his own trio. He has also been recorded on Southland with Sweet Emma's band, and on Atlantic's "Jazz at Preservation Hall" series with Jim Robinson's band. All of these recordings were made since 1960. Recently he has been playing only occasionally at Preservation Hall, as clarinetist with Peter Bocage's Creole Serenaders.

In addition to his playing he has also been very interested in the musicians' union and has been president of Local 496 for several years.

CROSBY, OCTAVE—piano

b. June 10, 1898, New Orleans

Octave Crosby began teaching himself to play the drums when he was about sixteen years old. For a while he played them on advertising wagons and with such dance bands as Louis Dumaine's. Later, when his mother bought a piano, he became interested in playing it, and, after a short period of self-instruction, he took lessons from Camilla Todd for about a year. In early New Orleans days not many boys played piano because it was considered a "sissy" instrument.

Later, he played again with Louis Dumaine, at the Bungalow at West End, but this time it was on the piano. He worked solo or with small pick-up groups at house parties and fish fries and was accompanist for silent movies at the Dauphine and Lyric theaters. He also made a tour with Gus Metcalf's Melody Band, playing carnival dates in Arkansas. Returning to New Orleans, he worked at the Bull's Club with Chris Kelly in the twenties and played with Buddy Petit's band on the lake boat *Susquehanna* for its Sunday excursions from West End to Mandeville. In 1926 he accompanied the Towles band, in which Herb Morand was trumpeter, on its three-month tour of Yucatan, Mexico.

Once back in New Orleans, he worked with several groups, including Kid Rena's band at the Budweiser taxi dance hall. He frequently substituted for Jeanette Kimball in the Celestin band, especially when it went on tour. In 1949, when the Celestin band was booked to play at the Paddock Lounge, Crosby became a permanent member of the group. He remained with the band for over a dozen years, and, at least part of the time, he was considered its leader.

He recorded with Celestin for Southland and other labels, and with Bill Matthews for Southland and Good Time Jazz. He was also recorded with his own band on a West Coast trip in the mid-fifties.

Octave's appearances at Preservation Hall are not frequent. When he plays, it is usually as a replacement in one of the regular bands such as the Kid Thomas Algiers Stompers, the Kid Sheik Storyville Ramblers, the Young Tuxedo band, and the George Lewis quartet.

FRAZIER, JOSIAH H. ("CIE")—drums

b. February 23, 1904, New Orleans

Cie Frazier was influenced by his older brother Sam, who played with New Orleans bands after World War I and into the early twenties.

After purchasing his first drum set in 1921, Cie took lessons from Louis Cottrell, Sr., and then around 1924 joined Bush Hall's Golden Rule Band, which included several of his relatives, Lawrence and Eddie Marrero, and Paul Barnes. Later he played with Ricard Alexis and Dwight Newman's Young Tuxedo Orchestra on the steamer *Idlewild*, with John Robichaux in the pit band at the Lyric Theater, and with Sidney Desvigne's Orchestra. In 1927 Cie recorded with Papa Celestin's Tuxedo Orchestra, and the following year he replaced Paul Barbarin in the A. J. Piron Orchestra, with which he remained until 1932.

In 1933 he joined the WPA band and also played spot jobs with other groups. In 1942 he enlisted in the Algiers Navy Band and in 1945, while he was still in the service, he recorded with Wooden Joe Nicholas. Following his discharge from the Navy he joined the Celestin band, and, after leaving this group in 1952, he played with Percy Humphrey, Sweet Emma Barrett, George Lewis, the George Williams Brass Band, and frequently with the Eureka Brass Band. In 1962, with the death of Alfred Williams, Cie became the regular drummer with the Eureka Brass Band, but after a year or so, he decided that the long parades were too much for him.

Cie was recorded several times in the sixties on Icon, Riverside, Atlantic, Pearl, San Jacinto, and GHB, as well as on both the Billie and DeDe Pierce and Sweet Emma Barrett LP's issued by Preservation Hall. He has made many tours with Billie and DeDe, and in 1966 toured England and Europe with Alvin Alcorn and Pops Foster.

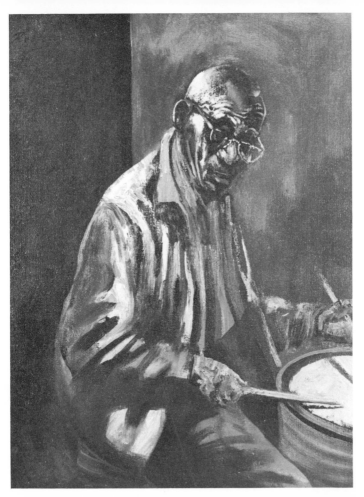

GALLAUD, LOUIS—piano

b. February 27, 1897, New Orleans

Louis Gallaud played at Preservation Hall frequently in its first years. In 1961, when he was in retirement and almost forgotten, the news spread that there was an interest in old-time musicians and Louis came by and demonstrated that he was still a piano player. He joined the union and played regularly with Kid Sheik's Storyville Ramblers, until the group broke up. From that time, until his retirement in 1966, he appeared occasionally at the Hall with Kid Thomas or as a replacement in one of the other bands.

Louis was born and raised in the "back o' town" section, and as a boy he marched in the second line at parades. He did not start playing the piano until he was eighteen years old and must be considered self-taught, although his friends Kid Rena, Kid Howard, the Morgan brothers, and Chris Kelly helped him.

His first job was for Ben Mulligan at Rampart and Gravier. Later he played in the District at Pete Lala's with A. J. Piron, and at Frank Early's, Tom Anderson's, and Harvey's. He also played at the Golden Slipper with Punch Miller and later led his own band, working at Milneburg and at Ruben's Restaurant at Little Woods. In the forties he worked at Luthjen's with Big Eye Louis Delisle and played occasional jobs with Wooden Joe Nicholas, Kid Rena, Chris Kelly, and Papa Celestin.

As a young man Gallaud listened to Jelly Roll Morton, Udell Wilson, and Fess Manetta and has a style which shows traces of these influences. Louis was recorded on the Icon label in 1962.

Rockmore
'63
march

GORMAN, ISRAEL—clarinet

b. March 4, 1895, Oakville, La. Plaquemines Parish
d. September 21, 1965, New Orleans

Israel Gorman started playing the cornet when he was fifteen years old, but after two or three years he switched to clarinet. His first teacher was Alphonse Picou, and later he took lessons from Lorenzo Tio, Sr., and from Lorenzo Tio, Jr. As a young man he was influenced by the clarinet styles of George Baquet and Johnny Dodds.

His first job was with George Jones's quartet at Tom Anderson's in 1915, and later he joined the Young Tuxedo Orchestra led by Maurice Durand. He frequently paraded with brass bands led by Manuel Perez, George Moret, Jack Carey, Chris Kelly, Buddy Petit, Peter Bocage, and Wooden Joe Nicholas. He also played spot jobs with Willie Cornish, Kid Rena, and Punch Miller.

During World War I he went overseas with an Army band, and on his return, he played with Wooden Joe Nicholas' Camelia Band on the lake steamer *Camelia.* Later he joined Toots Johnson's band headquartered at Baton Rouge, and after a couple of years he rejoined Buddy Petit's band, playing much of the time in Florida. Then followed several years of jobs with dance bands in Chicago and New York, until his return to New Orleans to join Papa Celestin's Tuxedo band. He also organized his own band and frequently played with Charlie Love at the Happy Landing.

There was a period in which he played with Percy Humphrey and Sweet Emma Barrett, as well as other popular bands around town. In the early Preservation Hall days he often played with Kid Sheik's Storyville Ramblers and with Kid Howard. It was during this period that he recorded on Icon.

'63
Roclamore
N.O.
march 30

ISRAEL
GORMAN

GUESNON, GEORGE ("CREOLE GEORGE")—banjo, guitar

b. May 25, 1907, New Orleans
d. May 5, 1968, New Orleans

Creole George Guesnon began playing professionally in 1927, when he joined Kid Clayton's Happy Pals at the Hummingbird cabaret. George had a few lessons from John Marrero, but for the most part perfected his own amazing technique on guitar and banjo. He was associated with the great names of his period, having played with Sam Morgan, Papa Celestin, Kid Rena, Chris Kelly, Buddy Petit, Punch Miller, George Lewis, and others. He recorded several blues records for Decca during the thirties, when he was seeking his fortune in New York and sharing an apartment with Jelly Roll Morton, who arranged some of his compositions.

In 1935 he went to Jackson, Mississippi, where he joined Little Brother Montgomery's orchestra and a year later the Rabbit Foot Minstrels. For two years he was featured as a banjo soloist, and during this time he extemporized endless lyrics which he sang to his own standard blues accompaniment. In 1940 he recorded again for Decca.

When World War II came, he joined the Merchant Marine and afterwards returned to New Orleans to play jobs with a variety of bands. He traveled with George Lewis to California and also to New York where they recorded for Blue Note. In 1959 George recorded for Icon and afterwards appeared on many traditional New Orleans jazz releases, including the Riverside "Living Legends" series and the Atlantic "Jazz at Preservation Hall" series.

Until his retirement in 1965, George appeared at Preservation Hall as leader of his own group or as sideman with other groups.

HANDY, JOHN ("CAPTAIN")—saxophone

b. June 24, 1900, Pass Christian, Miss.

John Handy's whole family was musical. His father played violin; his mother and sisters, piano; his brother Sylvester, bass; and his brother Julius, guitar.

John's first instrument was a chair round, which he learned to wet and rub to produce bass-like tones. When he was about seven he taught himself to play the mandolin and bass, but later he switched to guitar and then to drums and clarinet. He had his first job at the age of eleven when he and his brothers, working as a trio, played at a party in Pass Christian.

About 1918 he joined Tom Albert in New Orleans as clarinetist, and later played with Kid Rena, Buddy Petit, Jack Carey, Punch Miller, Chris Kelly, and John Casimir's brass band. Until 1928 or 1929, when he took up the alto sax, he was considered the king of the clarinetists.

He was recorded on Icon in 1962, and in 1967 on GHB, RCA Victor, and an English label. He has been particularly popular with foreign jazz enthusiasts in recent years. He has made tours of England and Europe, and he accompanied Kid Sheik on the 1967 tour of Japan.

He was dubbed "Captain" by "H. E." Minor, the banjo player. During a rehearsal with his own band, Handy left the stand for a few minutes, and when he came back, "H. E."said, "Hush up, here comes the Captain." The name stuck.

Handy's appearances at Preservation Hall are usually with Kid Sheik, and sometimes with his own group. He plays sax most of the time but occasionally plays his clarinet. His mastery of the blues and his exciting rhythm have earned him a devoted following.

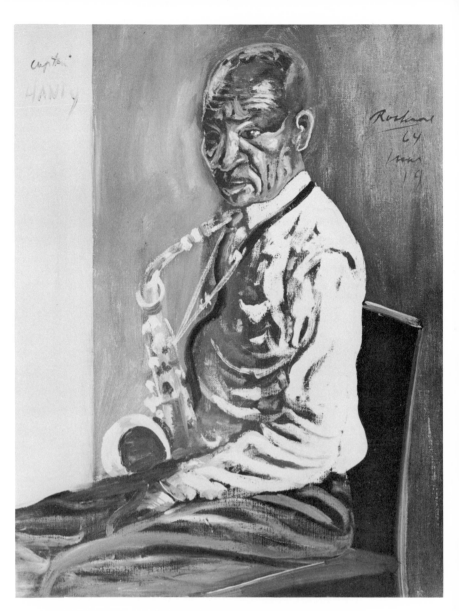

HENRY, OSCAR JOSEPH ("CHICKEN")—trombone, piano

b. June 8, 1888, New Orleans

When Chicken Henry was ten years old, his father got him a piano, and he studied this instrument about five years with Mrs. Louise Edler, who had played at the French Opera House. In 1906, after two years of high school at Straight University (now Dillard) , he learned the plastering trade, in which he worked all over the country, as well as in Cuba and Panama. In 1920 a lady gave him a trombone, which Charlie Clay taught him to play in Detroit. Later, while playing second trombone in Charlie Elgar's band, he studied theory with Frank L. Dry. He also studied tone with Alexander Valentine, a trombonist in Erskine Tate's orchestra at the Vendome Theater in Chicago.

In 1923 Oscar joined the Elks Concert Band in Chicago and went on its 1927 tour with a carnival show to Cleveland, New York, Philadelphia, Atlantic City, Baltimore, and Pittsburgh. He left the band in 1929, and in 1930 he went to Hot Springs, Arkansas, with the Tonic Triad Band, a large band from New Orleans, to play for a convention of the Woodmen of the World. He returned to New Orleans and joined the WPA band, which provided daily concerts for hospitals, convents, playgrounds, and other civic organizations. It was during this time that the men began calling him "Chick" or "Chicken Henry," and the name stuck.

In the early forties Chicken became the alternate trombonist with the Eureka Brass Band, filling in for Charles Sonny Henry or Albert Warner as needed, and when Sonny Henry died in 1960, Chicken replaced him. Chicken has also played with most of the town's other brass bands on occasion. In 1961 he was recorded on the Atlantic record of the Eureka Brass Band in the "Jazz at Preservation Hall" series, and in 1962 he also made a trip to Washington, D.C., with the band.

He has great pride in his plastering skill, even though retired from this craft, and says that he enjoyed sitting for Noel Rockmore because both are artists.

HOWARD, AVERY ("KID")—trumpet

b. April 22, 1908, New Orleans
d. March 28, 1966, New Orleans

The first band Kid Howard remembered hearing was Sam Morgan's.
He considered it great, and years later he realized his ambition of becoming
a member. When he was about twelve he started beating on a box
for a drum, and, although he had no lessons, he became a drummer within
a few years. About 1924 he organized his own band, but shortly thereafter
he became the regular drummer for Chris Kelly's band, which played
engagements at social clubs, parties, and dances and which was the
house band for the Tin Roof Club at Tchoupitoulas and Napoleon.
He also occasionally filled in on drums with Kid Rena, and during this
period Chris Kelly gave him some cornet lessons, which he later continued
with Professor Delmar.

After Kelly's death, Howard for the most part played trumpet with
his own band, but he also played frequently with the better known
New Orleans bands, such as Jack Carey's and Sam Morgan's. Jobs with
his own band included bookings at Milneburg, Bucktown, Spanish
Fort, and in country towns in Louisiana and Mississippi. In the late
twenties the band played on excursion trains to Chicago and occasionally
in Chicago itself. The group also worked at the Lavida and Fern taxi
dance halls and for about five years was the pit band at the Palace Theater.
Howard mastered an extensive repertoire ranging from Joplin rags out
of the old "red-back book" to hymns and popular numbers. He also
played frequently with several brass bands, including Eddie Jackson's
Original Tuxedo Band, the Young Tuxedo Band, the Eureka Brass Band,
and his own brass band.

When Preservation Hall opened Howard had been in retirement since
1960, but the opportunity to play again with enough regularity to maintain
his lip was very welcome to him, and before long he was bringing his own
group to the Hall.

HUMPHREY, PERCY G.—trumpet

b. January 13, 1905, New Orleans

Percy Humphrey comes from a famous musical family. His grandfather, Jim Humphrey, was one of the early "professors" who contributed to the formation of New Orleans music. Jim Humphrey's son Willie Humphrey, Sr., played clarinet, and the current generation of Humphrey brothers, Willie, Earl, and Percy, are all contributors to the continuity of New Orleans jazz.

Percy, who is the youngest of the three brothers, had his first job with Willie Cornish's band in the early twenties. In 1925 he organized his own dance orchestra and began playing occasional jobs with the Eureka Brass Band. In 1928 he joined Kid Howard's orchestra, playing on the L & N excursion trains, and in the thirties he had frequent jobs at the Alamo Club and the Lavida dance hall. He also went into the insurance business and continues to split his time between the two professions.

After World War II he became leader of the Eureka Brass Band. He also worked weekends at Manny's and other neighborhood halls, and often played with George Lewis. About 1950 he joined forces with Sweet Emma Barrett and began playing society parties and debutante balls. Later they played at the Old Absinthe House on Bourbon Street.

He has appeared at Preservation Hall frequently, both as leader of his own Crescent City Joy Makers and as sideman with Emma Barrett's Jazz Boys. He has recorded on Riverside, Southland, Pearl, San Jacinto, Icon, Arhoolie, and Atlantic. He has made many tours with both the Eureka Brass Band and with smaller groups, and has been featured on several television shows.

HUMPHREY, WILLIE J.—clarinet

b. December 29, 1900, New Orleans

Willie Humphrey is the oldest son of Willie E. Humphrey. He had violin lessons at the age of nine from his grandfather and played his first job with his father's band at a Poydras Market butcher's party. At fourteen he switched to clarinet and soon joined George McCullum's band and then the Silver Leaf Orchestra. He played a few jobs on the excursion steamer *Sidney* and in 1919 went to St. Louis for a season on the Strekfus boat *J. S.* In the fall Willie left the boat and went to Chicago, where he played with King Oliver at the World Series, George Fihle at the Deluxe Café, and with Freddie Keppard's band.

On his return to New Orleans in 1920 he joined Amos Riley's Tulane Band and also played with Frankie Duson at the Pythian Roof Garden. After a job with Zutty Singleton at Thom's Roadhouse, Willie organized his own band with Maurice Durand and later played as sideman with Kid Rena for about a year.

In 1925 he went back to St. Louis and worked on the *Capitol* under Fate Marable and later Dewey Jackson, with whom he made his first records. He returned to New Orleans in 1932, and during the depression he worked for a while in the WPA band. About 1933 he began teaching music and still continues this activity. In the mid-thirties he joined Mills Blue Rhythm Band on a theatre tour and recorded with Red Allen when the group reached New York. On his return to New Orleans he worked with various musicians and bands, among them Louis Dumaine, Steve Lewis, and in the NOLA Band with Peter Lacaze and Eddie Jackson.

During World War II Humphrey served in a Navy band. During his career he has played in several New Orleans brass bands, the first of which was the old Excelsior in which he played E-flat clarinet under George Moret. In late years he has been a member of the Eureka Brass Band.

In the early fifties Willie worked regularly with Paul Barbarin's band but later in the fifties he became a member of Sweet Emma's group. At Preservation Hall he has appeared frequently with Sweet Emma and occasionally with his own Hot Four. He has recorded on Riverside, Good Time Jazz, Southland, and Atlantic. He went with Billie and DeDe Pierce on their 1967 tour of Europe and on their United States college tour.

JAMES, JOE—piano

b. 1901, Algiers, La.
d. 1964, New Orleans

Joe James started picking the banjo at fourteen. He would come across the river to New Orleans to study with Professor Dave Perkins at Perkin's home on Sixth Street in the Garden District. Dave Perkins was one of the famous old music masters, whose students included Baby Dodds, Red Clark, and other jazz luminaries. Lessons were fifty cents and well worth it.

Joe's next instrument was guitar, and it was not until he was about eighteen that he became interested in the piano. His experience on guitar and banjo helped him to play by ear, and he was able to "chord" and "fake." Later he had a few lessons from Professor Manuel Manetta. When he started working with bands he preferred to play piano because, as he said, "I used to drink a lot and didn't care for packing all that junk around."

From 1925 until his death in 1964, Joe James played with Kid Thomas Valentine's band and appeared on all of the Kid Thomas albums. A rare vocal of "Stingaree Blues" is on the New Orleans Jazz Society LP.

There is little doubt that the sound and style of the Kid Thomas band was directly related to Joe James's piano style, and Thomas has had great difficulty finding a replacement to continue the stomping, driving, primitive performances for which his band is known.

JAMES, LOUIS DOUGLAS, SR.—bass

b. April 9, 1890, Johnson Ridge, La.
d. October 26, 1967, New Orleans

Louis James came from a musical family. His four brothers played guitar, clarinet, sax, and bass. Louis' first instrument was a "heel and head-comb," which is an idiomatic way of saying he stamped his foot for rhythm while blowing through tissue paper stretched across a comb. This is a general musical form among southern children. When Louis was eight he started playing the mandolin, and later the violin. By the time he was twelve he was playing the clarinet, and at fifteen he was playing the sax. The clarinet was his principle instrument until he began playing the bass, when he was almost twenty-five. From that time the bass was his mainstay. On all of these instruments he was self-taught.

Louis' first job, when he was about ten, was with his own group in Johnson Ridge, Louisiana. Then in 1915 he came to New Orleans and in the late twenties recorded there with Louis Dumaine's band. Returning to the Thibodaux area, he played for a while with the Gabriel brothers' band but then he came back to New Orleans and took jobs with such famous leaders as John Robichaux, Manuel Manetta, Percy Humphrey, Kid Howard, and others. He also made a trip to Florida with Albert French's band and traveled with Desdunes to Mississippi and Alabama engagements.

He recorded with Herb Morand in the late forties, and in the sixties he recorded on Riverside, Icon, and Mono. He appeared at Preservation Hall with Emma Barrett's band until his retirement in 1965.

JEFFERSON, ANDREW B.—drummer

b. November 24, 1912, New Orleans

Andrew Jefferson began his musical career as a drummer at parties
and fish frys, playing with such barrelhouse pianists as Jimmy Carter
and Stack O'Lee. Later he formed his own little band called the "Yo Yo
Boys," and soon he was playing with many of New Orleans' best
musicians, including Kid Rena, with whom he had an extended engagement at the Cadillac in the early forties. Beginning with the one which
he and Kid Clayton organized, he has played with practically all of the
New Orleans brass bands of the last quarter century. He toured with
the Olympia Brass Band to Washington, D.C., and to Europe in 1967.
At Preservation Hall he has appeared frequently with Peter Bocage
and occasionally with other bands.

JILES, ALBERT, JR.—drums

b. November 27, 1905, Thibodaux, La.
d. September 3, 1964, New Orleans

Albert Jiles's father, Albert Jiles, Sr., was drummer in Joe Gabriel's Thibodaux jazz band. Albert, Jr., showed musical interest as a five-year-old, and when the family moved to New Orleans ten years later, his uncle Clay Jiles, of the Excelsior Brass Band, arranged for lessons with Professor Chaligny.

Albert's first professional job was with pianist Herman Weiss. He later joined a group including Lawrence Toca, Bill Hamilton, and Melvin Frank. It is interesting that the rates for this quartet in the early twenties were three dollars per man for a two-hour advertising job and five or six dollars per man for a four-hour dance. Albert's first regular job was with Chris Kelly. He also played with Rene Parker's Oneida Jazz Band, a six-piece band using stock arrangements.

During the depression Jiles took jobs in the waterfront dives on Decatur Street, working with George Lewis, Billie and DeDe Pierce, Alton Purnell, and Kid Howard. After the death of Sam Morgan, Albert worked with the Morgan band under the leadership of Isaiah Morgan. He also played with Kid Rena at Economy Hall and Perseverance Hall, with George Lewis at the Silver Star on St. Bernard and St. Claude, and with Albert Walters at the Last Round-Up on Bienville and Dauphine. Later he joined Papa Celestin, and when the band broke up, he worked with Kid Clayton and John Handy, and at the Dandy Inn with Albert Burbank. Then in the fifties Jiles and Charlie Love had a band on the lake front at the Happy Landing for about five years.

In 1949 Bill Russell recorded Jiles, and in 1961 Jiles recorded on the Riverside "Living Legend" series. After Chinee Foster's death, until his own death, Jiles worked regularly at Preservation Hall with Billie and DeDe Pierce.

JOHNSON, EDWARD T. ("NOON")—bazooka, guitar, tuba

b. August 24, 1901, New Orleans

As a boy Noon Johnson made his own instrument by driving nails in a fence. He strung wire from old broom handles between the rails and played the strings with sticks in a xylophone fashion. Then at fourteen he started to play the ukulele and harmonica. Later he scrapped a brass bed and fitted two tubes to make a slide; this instrument produced a bass-like sound. He added a little black horn from an old Grafonola for a bell and a brass plumbing union for a mouthpiece. He called it a "funnelphone."

In 1924 Walter Coquille, the "Mayor of Bayou PomPom," took Noon to play a convention at Biloxi. Bob Burns, who was on the convention program, saw the funnelphone, and by 1929 Noon's brainchild, rechristened "bazooka," was nationally known through the Bob Burns show.

Noon worked with three or four pieces—a guitar and occasionally a kazoo, the harmonica, tubaphone, banjo, and drums or bass—and with his clowning won some amateur contests. His group was booked for tours as far as Nashville. Black Walter Nelson gave him instruction on the guitar and later Noon worked as a guitarist on the streets and in restaurants and clubs. He also mastered the tenor banjo and later the tuba, which he played in parades with the Kid Howard, Abby Williams, and Young Tuxedo brass bands. He made a blues recording with Bunk Johnson and occasionally replaced Lawrence Marrero in the George Lewis band.

In the days before Preservation Hall, Noon and his trio often stopped to play at the art gallery next to Pat O'Brien's, and later, in the early days of the Hall, he led his own group as one of the regularly appearing bands, and was a member of the Preservation Hall tour which went to Cleveland in 1961. He still has his old "brass bed" funnelphone, but he usually carries a light-weight model. He occasionally appears at Preservation Hall with Percy Humphrey's band.

JONES, CHESTER—drums

b. March 13, 1913, on the lower coast of Algiers, Orleans Parish, La.

Chester Jones's father was a cornetist. When Chester was a year old, his family moved to the Treme district, where he has lived ever since. His home was near Hopes Hall on Liberty Street and Economy Hall on Ursulines. Often the bands that worked at the halls would play a few numbers outside before the dances began, and Chester learned that if he carried the drums inside for the musicians, he could stay and listen. He was able to hear Chris Kelly and Kid Rena and to watch such drummers as Black Benny, Face-O, Alfred Williams, and Big Rudolph. Chester started in "kid bands," playing the drums, as well as kazoos and slide whistles. He also played a melodeon at home and in church. He was self-taught and never did learn to read music. From time to time, drummer Edgar Mosley let him "sit in" on his jobs.

Chester's first job was at Grand Isle with Homer Eugene on guitar and Harrison Verrett on piano. At this time he was also a boxer. At prize fights a band usually played between bouts and Chester would often sit beside the band, when he wasn't fighting, to watch the drummer.

From 1933 until 1938 Chester worked with Kid Howard's Brass Band. He recalls the band playing for funerals starting from the Caldonia Club, where the back room was used for wakes. He also worked with George Lewis, Albert Burbank, Sidney Desvigne, Papa Celestin, and others at such locations as San Jacinto Hall, the Rhythm Club, the Italian Hall, and the Paddock Lounge. After Alfred Williams' death Chester became regular drummer for the Eureka Brass Band.

At Preservation Hall he plays with several groups, but usually with Sweet Emma Barrett's band or with Kid Sheik, with whom he toured Japan in 1967.

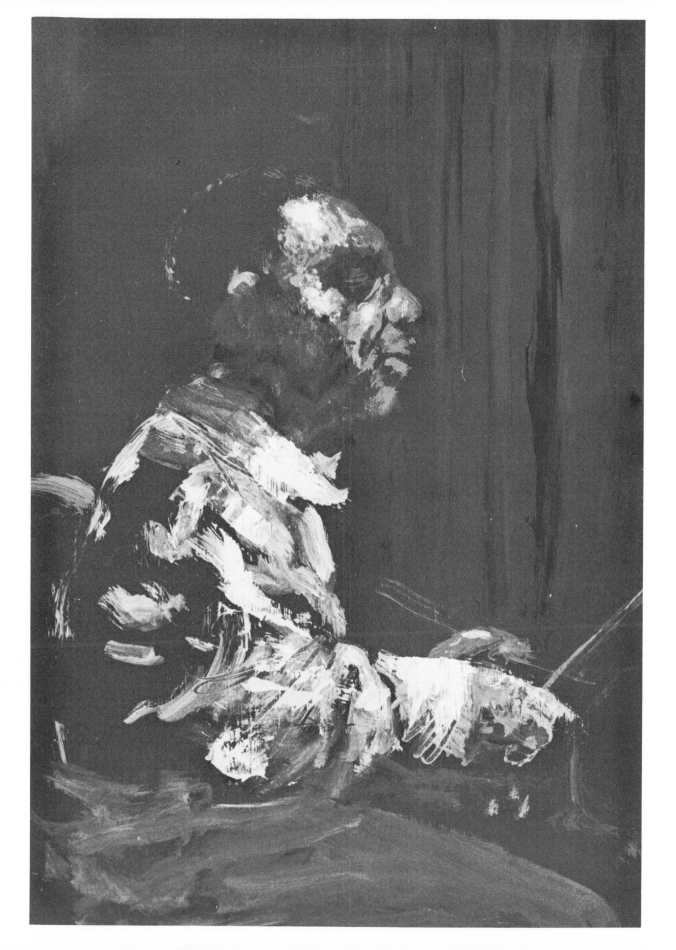

JOSEPH, ("PAPA") JOHN—bass

b. November 27, 1874, Jamestown, St. James Parish, La.
d. January 22, 1965, New Orleans

John Joseph began playing music at eleven years old. He learned violin, mandolin, bass, clarinet, and sax. His father, brothers, and other members of his family were musicians, and his first job was with his brother Nelson, two uncles, and bass player and violinist Wellman Braud.

In 1906 John came to New Orleans, where he worked with Edward Clem, Pinchback Touro, Lawrence Duhe, Louis Dumaine, Louis James, Tom Benton, Joe Johnson, Shots Madison, Manuel Manetta, and Buddy Petit at such places as the Longshoremen's Hall, Masonic Hall, Odd Fellows Hall, Mississippi Valley Hall, Funky Butt Hall, Big 25, Sans Souci, the Pythian Roof Garden, and many other old-time halls and clubs. He also had a barber shop on First Street, and, across the street from it he ran dances for which he hired King Oliver, Kid Ory, John Robichaux, and others. In 1913 he left New Orleans and played with the Holmes Band in Lutcher, where he learned to read music. He also played with the Claiborne Williams band of Donaldsonville. Henry Baltimore, Claiborne Williams' bass player, was his ideal.

In the fifties Papa John was a strolling musician, often with Noon Johnson's trio or with Lemon Nash. These groups often played in Pat O'Brien's patio on Sunday afternoons. Then they would stop at the art gallery next door to warm up and get any tips which could be obtained there. Papa John also played with Punch Miller in sessions at the gallery, and these appearances were part of the stimulus which led to the forming of Preservation Hall.

After Preservation Hall opened, Papa John joined the union for the first time at the age of eighty-six. He went to Cleveland with Kid Sheik's Storyville Ramblers and recorded for Atlantic in 1962, and in 1963 he went to Japan with George Lewis. After his return he played frequently at the Hall with several different groups. His death while performing in concert at Preservation Hall was a fitting terminus to his notable career.

KIMBALL, NARVIN HENRY—banjo, bass

b. March 2, 1909, New Orleans

Narvin Kimball's father, Henry Kimball, was one of the all-time great jazz musicians on string bass and sousaphone. Narvin made his first stringed instrument from a cigar box before he was twelve. Later he bought a ukelele, and in 1924 his father gave him a banjo, which he played the following year with his high school band, led by Valmore Victor. Willie Foster took an interest in the lad and gave him some lessons on banjo, and Paul Moliere asked him to play with his family band, which rehearsed weekly. At the age of seventeen Narvin made a tour up the river with Fate Marable on the steamer *Capitol*. In the fall the boat docked in New Orleans for the winter, and Narvin stayed on with the band while completing his high school education. After graduation he attended New Orleans University (now Dillard) for two years and was a member of the university band, directed by Mrs. Sigismund Walker. It is noteworthy that Jerry Green was a fellow bandsman. In 1927 Narvin joined Sidney Desvigne's orchestra and later became a member of Papa Celetin's Original Tuxedo Orchestra, in which he played both banjo and guitar. About this time one of his compositions, "Don't Let Old Age Creep Up On You," was recorded by the Ink Spots on Decca.

Narvin discontinued playing in 1935 because music jobs became so scarce during the depression, but in 1940 he rejoined Desvigne's orchestra and stayed with it until its dissolution in 1947. In 1945 he performed on bass with Louis Armstrong as a feature of the National Jazz Foundation show in New Orleans. In 1948 he joined Fred Minor, Alvin Alcorn, and Louis Barbarin in a quartet called the Four Tones. This group disbanded in 1951, and Kimball became bassist for Herbert Leary's orchestra until 1959. Late in 1959 his own band, Kimball's Gentlemen of Jazz, started playing the Wednesday night relief job at the Paddock Lounge, and for a year and a half they played weekends at the Old Absinthe House.

Narvin is heard at Preservation Hall frequently as sideman for Sweet Emma or Billie and DeDe Pierce and occasionally as leader of his own group.

LEWIS, GEORGE—clarinet

b. July 13, 1900, New Orleans

George Lewis grew up near Hopes Hall, where he listened to music
almost every night. When he was seven his mother gave him a
quarter to buy a toy violin, hoping to keep him off the streets, but George
bought a tin fife which he quickly learned to play. It was not until he
was sixteen that he saved up the four dollars necessary to purchase
a real clarinet at a Rampart Street pawn shop. Within a year he was
playing well enough to join the Black Eagles of Mandeville, where he
spent the summer. It was here that he heard the Fritz family band and
was influenced by clarinetist Isadore Fritz. He then began playing
with Buddy Petit's Black and Tan Band, and, when Buddy and Earl
Humphrey formed a new band, George joined as clarinetist. He later
organized his own band with Red Allen on trumpet, and after a year or
so, he began playing with other leaders, including Kid Punch, Chris
Kelly, and Kid Rena. In the early thirties he played in the Evan Thomas
band with Bunk Johnson and Chinee Foster, who were also members.
Through the years George has played in many parades and funerals
with brass bands, in addition to dance jobs.

During the depression he worked as a stevedore during the day and
played music nights. Occasionally he played with Billie and DeDe
Pierce and many other musicians who later found themselves reunited at
Preservation Hall. Sometimes he led a trio playing as long as eight
hours for a dollar. In 1942 he recorded with Bunk Johnson. This led to
a series of recordings which made him the most recorded New Orleans
musician. A few years later, in 1945, he went to New York with Bunk's
band and soon became the most celebrated New Orleans traditionalist.
Later he toured with his own band from coast to coast, and in 1958
made the first of several trips to England and the continent.

George has appeared frequently at Preservation Hall from its earliest
days, and since 1963 his Preservation Hall band has made extensive
tours of Japan to perform and record.

George Lewis

Rockmore
'63

mar. 13

new orleans

MATTHEWS, BILL—trombone

b. May 9, 1899, Algiers, La.
d. June 3, 1964, New Orleans

Bill Matthews' father, William Matthews, Sr., played organ and piano, and his two older brothers, Ramos and "Bebe," were respected jazz drummers. Bill got started on drums when he was about seventeen and worked occasionally with the Excelsior Brass Band. A couple of years later, he got his first job as snare drummer with the George McCullum band, and between 1915 and 1920 he worked with Buddy Petit, Jack Carey, John Robichaux, Kid Rena, A. J. Piron, Sam Morgan, Sidney Desvigne, Jack "Pie Eater" Williams, King Oliver's Onward Brass Band, and Henry Allen's Brass Band. In 1921 Bill went on a vaudeville tour of the North with Mack and Mack, and later was with Charles Creath at Tom Turpin's Jazzland in St. Louis. In 1922 he started to play the trombone, taking lessons from Vic Gaspard. As a trombonist, he went on the road with Nat Towles and toured with Jelly Roll Morton.

He returned to New Orleans in 1925, on board the steamer *Inland Queen* and began playing at West End. Other jobs about this time included the Crescent dance hall and Tranchina's at Spanish Fort. In 1927 he became a regular member of Celestin's Original Tuxedo Band, which played at the Paddock Lounge. When Celestin gave up the job, Bill organized his own jazz band and remained there as its leader about a decade. During this time he played with the Young Tuxedo Brass Band, the Eureka Brass Band, and the George Williams Brass Band. Later he led orchestras in other Bourbon Street clubs, which included Sid Davila's Mardi Gras Lounge.

When Preservation Hall opened, Bill became one of the regular leaders, frequently with his own group and occasionally with other bands as a replacement. He has been recorded with Celestin, George Lewis, Paul Barbarin, and his own band.

MILLER, ERNEST ("KID PUNCH")—trumpet

b. June 10, 1894, Raceland, La.

Ernest Miller got his nickname from relatives and friends, who called him Punch and his twin sister, Judy, names which followed them all through life. Punch first played bass drum and then cornet in a kid brass band in Jefferson Parish. The kids often met excursion trains which frequently brought New Orleans bands through, and, on one occasion, Punch managed to sit in with Bunk Johnson's band during a stop at the depot.

During World War I Punch became a bugler in the army with the rank of corporal. After his discharge he settled in New Orleans and joined Jack Carey's band. In 1923 he formed his own band and soon had one of the most popular groups in the city. In 1927, however, he left New Orleans and made Chicago his headquarters for the next twenty years, playing as sideman with Freddie Keppard and others, or as leader of his own Delegates of Pleasure. During this period he recorded with half a dozen Chicago bands, made frequent tours with Billy and Mary Mack's Merrymakers, and traveled with dance bands led by Jelly Roll Morton, Fate Marable, and others. Punch found the traveling jobs enjoyable and spent more and more time on the road, touring with circuses, rodeos, minstrel shows, and carnivals. On a trip to New York in 1947 he recorded for Century and appeared on radio.

Punch returned to New Orleans in 1956 after doing a stint with Claxton's Musical Review. He looked up his old friend Beansie Fauria, who introduced him to the art gallery sessions which took place occasionally on St. Peter Street. Punch formed a band and soon was playing at the art gallery every Tuesday and Thursday night. These regular appearances helped lead to Preservation Hall's development. People started to come on other nights hoping to hear music, and often there wasn't any, but the fact that a demand for traditional jazz existed was a discovery for a town which had turned its back on its only creative contribution.

Punch was recorded in 1959 on Folkways and in 1960 on Icon. After Preservation Hall got underway he also recorded for Atlantic and Imperial. He made a trip to Cleveland with a Preservation Hall band and was trumpeter on the first George Lewis tour of Japan.

MILLER, JAMES EDWARD ("SING")—piano

b. June 17, 1913, New Orleans

James "Sing" Miller comes from a musical family. His uncle, Edward Johnson, played bass, his father played the piccolo, and his younger sister played the piano. Sing got his nickname as a child because he liked to sing. His first instrument was a violin tuned like a ukelele, and later he took up the banjo and the string bass.

Sing's first job was on banjo at the Okeh Lounge in 1927, and later he joined Kid Howard's band. His career on piano started about 1928. Except for some organ lessons which he had at school, he was self-taught on the piano, although he was influenced by Steve Lewis, Jeanette Kimball, Isadore Washington, and Stack O'Lee, a blues pianist, who was a neighbor. About this time Sing started playing fish fries and yard parties, informal affairs which were usually benefits for a sick person or a church or just to help the householder pay his rent.

In the thirties Sing joined Earl Foster's quartet, an association which lasted into the mid-forties, but he also played occasional jobs with Chris Kelly at the Bull's Club, Kid Rena at the Cadillac, and with other bands at the Lavida and Budweiser dance halls. Over the years his jobs included a season with a tent show traveling as far as Tennessee, a long engagement at the Carnival Club at Dryades and Euterpe streets, six years at the Club Plantation in Bogalusa, four years at Seymour's Coconut Grove across the river, three years with Kid Clayton's band at Mamma Lou's, several years at the College Inn in Thibodaux, and a stint with the James brothers in Houma. Then after Joe James's death, Sing joined Kid Thomas' band, with which he recorded.

Sing appears frequently at Preservation Hall with Percy Humphrey and Kid Sheik.

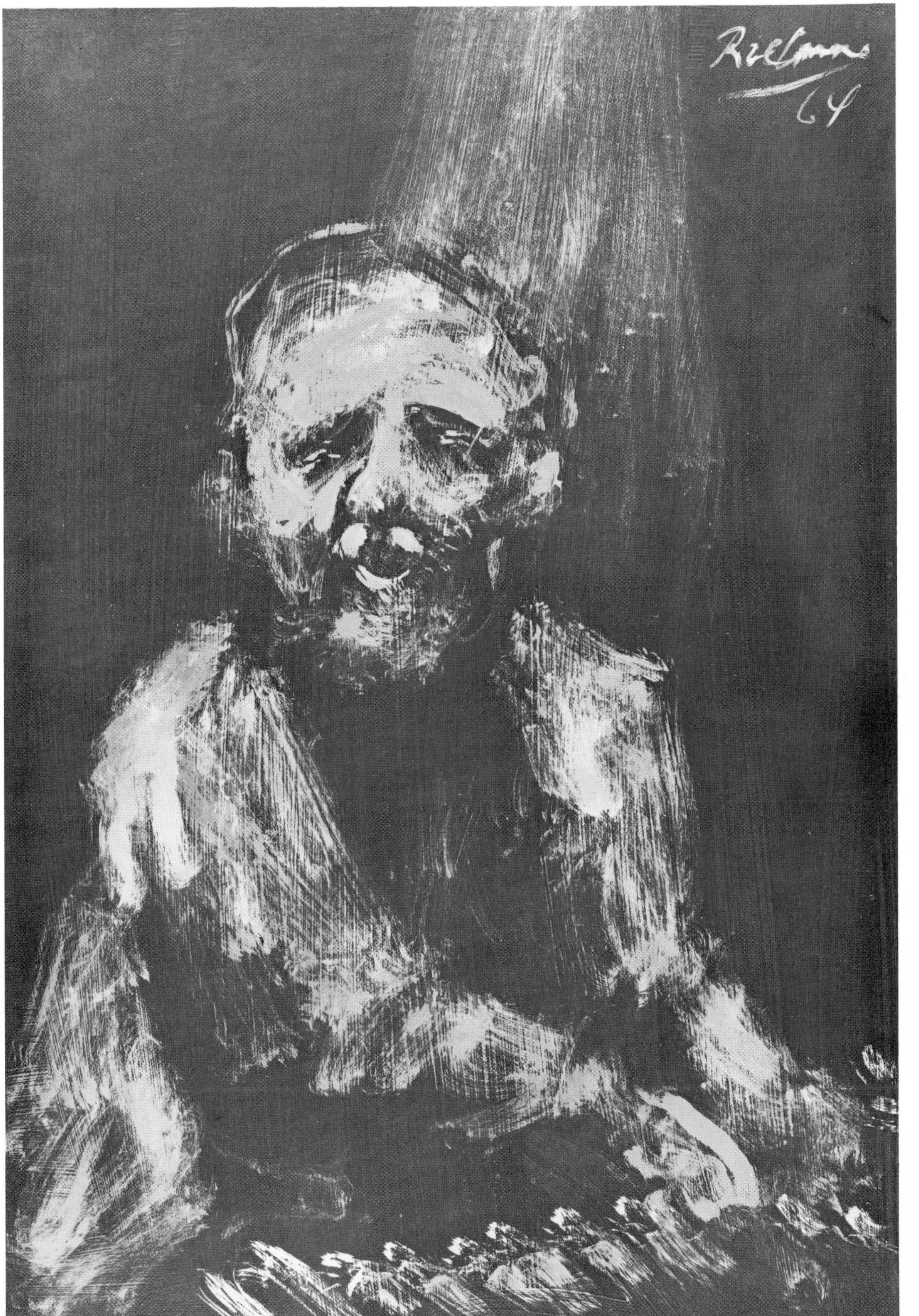

MOLIERE, FRANK ("LITTLE DADDY")—piano

b. October 4, 1914, New Orleans

Frank Moliere was born and raised on Burgundy and St. Anthony streets. His first interest in music came from his cousin Paul Moliere, a cornetist who taught DeDe Pierce, and his cousin Ernest Moliere, a clarinetist. Frank taught himself to play the piano. He says his grandmother used to lock it because he was making "just noise," but he had a key made and would play when she was out of the house.

In the thirties Frank played with Isaiah Morgan in Mississippi, and with Kid Howard, Thomas Jefferson, Dave Oxley, and others at the Palace Theater in New Orleans for about four years. In 1942 Frank joined the Army Signal Corps and saw overseas duty during World War II. After his discharge in 1946 he played with Earl Williams, mostly in Mobile, but also at the Dream Room and at the Slave Bar on Bourbon Street. About this time he took piano lessons at Grunewald's, and it took him three months to learn to read music. He says this helped him a great deal. After about a year with Williams, he joined Danny White's Cavaliers at the Sand Club on St. Charles Avenue, where he played for two years. Then he worked with Smilin' Joe at the Famous Door for a couple of years, and after that with Clement Tervalon at the Paddock for four years, replacing Octave Crosby on piano. Following these engagements he took jobs wherever he could, playing mostly as a single at piano bars.

In 1965 he joined the George Lewis Preservation Hall Band and also appeared with George Lewis in his engagements at the Red Garter. When this series of concerts was over, he stayed on at the Red Garter as featured pianist.

MOLIERE '66
Rochette

MORGAN, ANDREW—clarinet and saxophone

b. March 19, 1903, Pensacola, Fla.

   Andrew Morgan is one of the famous musical Morgan brothers, and
was surrounded by music in his early life. His older brothers Sam
and Isaiah were trumpeters, and his younger brother Al was soon to play
string bass. Andrew started on the clarinet but later switched to tenor
sax.
   Although he was born in Florida, Andrew is considered to be a
New Orleans musician. His first job was with the Young Superior Brass
Band in 1924. Then in 1925 his brother Isaiah took him into the
Young Morgan Band, and in April, 1927, he was recorded by Columbia
as part of the Sam Morgan Jazz Band, which included Jim Robinson on
trombone. In 1930 Andrew joined Mike DeLay's band, and when
jobs became scarce, he joined the WPA band. Later in the thirties he
began playing with Kid Thomas' band across the river in Algiers. Then
in 1944 he played at the Brown Derby dance hall with Kid Rena's band,
which included Alphonse Picou. During the mid-forties through the
fifties he jobbed around town, frequently working in various brass bands.
He also played a variety of engagements at the lake front, including
Mama Lou's with Herb Morand and later Peter Bocage.
   Andrew plays at Preservation Hall with Kid Sheik's Storyville Ramblers,
and occasionally with Peter Bocage or one of the other groups. In
1963 he played with the Billie and DeDe Pierce band in Houston for
the Contemporary Art Association.
   He is a pleasing showman, and one of his tricks is to hold a sustained
note on his clarinet or sax through several choruses of the "St. Louis Blues."

NELSON, LOUIS—trombone

b. September 17, 1902, New Orleans

As a child Louis Nelson was given musical instruction by his mother, who was an accomplished pianist and a graduate of the Boston Conservatory. Louis began his jazz career playing with Joe Gabriel's band in Thibodaux, and in his early years he played with the Original Tuxedo Orchestra, Kid Rena's band, and occasionally with pick-up groups. Later he joined Sidney Desvigne's orchestra and played with it for fifteen years, five of which were on riverboats. It was with this band that he developed a style of playing the melodic line on the trombone which is still distinctively his. During the depression he was in the WPA music program, under the direction of Pinchback Touro and Louis Dumaine, and in 1944 he joined the Kid Thomas band.

Nelson was among the musicians who came regularly to the art gallery sessions on St. Peter Street, and his part in these sessions helped develop the enthusiasm which led to Preservation Hall. It was also through these appearances that New Orleans musicians became reacquainted with him. For years he had played across the river, and to many musicians he was a real discovery. George Lewis found his mellow tone well suited to the ensemble sound he desired and started using him regularly. Nelson made three trips with Lewis to Japan and was recorded there by King and by Victor. At home he has been recorded on Riverside with Percy Humphrey and with Kid Thomas and also appears on three of Atlantic's "Jazz at Preservation Hall" releases.

Nelson has developed a large following, based on his dignified appearance as well as his musicianship. He excels at playing harmony, vamping, or playing tailgate. His presence in a small band gives it a big band sound.

OXLEY, DAVE, SR.—drums

b. May 1, 1910, New Orleans

When Dave Oxley was about six he started beating on doorsteps with chair rounds. He joined the second line when the brass bands passed, and he helped his mother at fish fries by playing the drums to the accompaniment of a phonograph. His ambition to be a drummer was set. He started on a snare drum when he was fourteen and within a year he quit school, went to work at the dry docks, and bought a complete set of drums. Although he was influenced by Red Happy, who played at the Lyric Theatre, Dave must be considered self-taught.

His first job was with Punch Miller at Milneburg. He also played occasionally with Chris Kelly and later with Kid Howard. He joined a vaudeville show on the T.O.B.A. circuit, playing Chicago, New York, Atlanta, and Cincinnati. While in the show he developed a specialty drum solo and got a raise to twenty-five dollars a week. He also toured with other shows and carnivals for about seven years. Returning to New Orleans he worked with Joe Robichaux at the Pig Pen, the Key Club, the Paddock, and the Famous Door, and with Fat Pichon at the Absinthe House. He went back on the road in 1937 with Bessie Smith in "Broadway Rastus." It was on this tour that Bessie was fatally injured in an automobile accident. Dave recalls that the last number she sang in her final concert was, "This Is My Last Affair." Then in 1940 Dave was with Ida Cox for almost a year in a show called "Darktown Scandals Revue," in which Lonnie Johnson also played. During the war Dave led a ten-piece Army band.

Dave was in retirement until George Lewis brought him to Preservation Hall. Within a few weeks he had regained his skill and is now one of the regular drummers to appear there. Audiences love his singing as well as his playing.

PAUL, EMANUEL—violin, banjo, saxophone

b. February 2, 1904, New Orleans

At seventeen, Emanuel Paul began playing the violin in a church band, which included Sam Dutry, who played clarinet. Later, Emanuel took up the banjo in order to play some dance jobs. A cousin who played piano, James Paul, organized a group with which Emanuel played banjo until 1934. In 1935 he joined the ERA band led by Louis Dumaine, and in 1936 he joined the WPA band, in which he played soprano sax but later switched to tenor sax. He then joined a trio with Albert French on banjo and Sam Mossey on drums and played at the Shadowland, and at that time he joined the union. Between 1934–39 he played with John Robichaux at country dances.

About 1940 he joined a band led by Dominique "T-Boy" Remy, which played on Napoleon Avenue, and it was through "T-Boy" that he joined the Eureka Brass Band. Since that time, Emanuel has become the mainstay of the band, as his use of the tenor sax takes the place of the baritone horn. His solo on "Westlawn" dirge is one of the most beautiful passages to be heard in a New Orleans funeral parade.

About 1945 he began playing occasionally with Kid Thomas at the Moulin Rouge, and since the opening of Preservation Hall, Paul is heard there with Kid Thomas' Algiers Stompers.

Emanuel recorded with the Eureka Brass Band in 1951 on Pax, in 1958 on Folkways, and in 1962 on Atlantic. He has also recorded with the Kid Thomas band, and in 1965 and 1967 he toured Europe and was recorded in England.

PAVAGEAU, ALCIDE ("SLOW DRAG")—bass

b. March 7, 1888, New Orleans

Alcide "Slow Drag" Pavageau is probably the most photographed Preservation Hall musician. He does so many interesting things that everyone who has a camera wants his picture. As "official grand marshal of the second line," marching between the band and its followers, he struts down the street, dressed in old-fashioned tails, wearing a black derby, and carrying a bright red gaily festooned parasol.

His father, a first cousin of voodoo queen Marie Laveau, played guitar, and Drag started on this instrument when he was fifteen. Later he took guitar lessons from Ulysses Picou and joined a "rooty tooty" band which busked on Basin Street and occasionally played for dances and parties. His real claim to fame, however, was as champion at dance competitions held at Hopes Hall, Economy Hall, Globe Hall, and others. He excelled at the schottish, mazurka, waltz, quadrille, cakewalk, and of course, the slow drag.

About 1927 he made a three-string bass and soon mastered it, playing with practically all of the good bands in New Orleans, including Emile Barnes, Buddy Petit, Herb Morand, and Elmer Talbert. In 1943 he joined George Lewis, with whom he has since principally been identified. He made a trip to New York in 1945 with Bunk Johnson and to Europe in 1958 with George Lewis. He also toured the United States with Lewis. Since 1961 Slow Drag has been acting as grand marshal of the Eureka Brass Band.

At Preservation Hall Slow Drag has been heard with several groups, including Johnny Wiggs, George Lewis, Sweet Emma, and Punch Miller. He has been recorded dozens of times on a variety of labels.

PENN, SAMUEL HUGHES—drums

b. September 15, 1902, Morgan City, La.

Samuel Penn's first bass drum was made from a tub, his snare drum from a cheese box, and his sticks from chair rounds. As a young fellow in Morgan City he learned a little from Jake Johnson and became drummer in his band. He must be considered self-taught as most of his skill was gained by listening to and watching other drummers. He took advantage of every opportunity to sit in with the New Orleans bands that played in Morgan City, if they would put up with him. From the time he was thirteen until he moved to New Orleans at twenty-two, he was the regular snare drummer with a country brass band made up of musicians from Morgan City, Berwick, and surrounding settlements.

In New Orleans he found work with the Jules Barnes band, and after a couple of years he joined Buddy Petit, with whom he was associated until Buddy's death in 1931. The band played the usual run of dances and lawn parties, as well as appearing at the Fair Grounds, at National Park ball games, and with advertising wagons. It also went on train excursions and a tour of Texas. After the band broke up, Sammy played with Punch Miller at the Patterson Hotel on South Rampart Street and with Chris Kelly and Kid Rena.

Sammy Penn has for many years been a singer as well as a drummer. To amplify his voice, he has used a megaphone or sometimes his snare drum, which he holds to his cheek so that in effect the drum acts as a resonator. This gives an unusual effect, especially when he is drumming with his other hand.

For over twenty years Sammy has been a drummer for Kid Thomas' band and appears as drummer on all of Kid Thomas' records and at Preservation Hall whenever the band plays there.

PIERCE, JOSEPH LA CROIX ("DEDE")—cornet

b. February 18, 1904, New Orleans

PIERCE, WILHELMINA ("BILLIE")—piano

b. June 8, 1907, Marianna, Fla.

When Billie Pierce was fifteen and living in Pensacola, Bessie Smith, "Empress of the Blues," played a week's engagement at the local theatre. Bessie's regular accompanist, Clarence Williams, took sick and Billie, who already had a local reputation, replaced him with notable distinction. The Bessie Smith influence on Billie's vocal style since the days of this early triumph is still evident.

After travels in Florida and Alabama as an entertainer in shows and as a band pianist, Billie came to New Orleans in 1929 to temporarily replace her sister Sadie Goodson in Buddy Petit's band on the lake steamer *Madison*. Billie stayed on in New Orleans, and during the depression she worked in the rowdy honky-tonks along the Decatur Street waterfront for a dollar a night. While she was working with George Lewis in one of these tonks, DeDe Pierce joined the four-piece band. Three weeks later, on March 28, 1935, Billie and DeDe were married.

DeDe had learned trumpet from Professor Chaligny and Kid Rena. He first played professionally with Arnold DePass' band. DeDe's people were French-speaking, and the Creole folk songs which DeDe arranged and sang, such as "Sallee Dame" and "Eh La Bas," added spice to his repertoire.

Except for DeDe's brass band jobs, he and Billie almost always worked together after their marriage. Their longest engagement extended over a period of a dozen years at Luthjen's, a small neighborhood dance hall down on Marais Street. Many of New Orleans' best musicians played with them at times, among them Alphonse Picou, Big Eye Louis, and Emile and Paul Barnes.

In the fifties both Billie and DeDe were plagued with ill health. DeDe's eyesight failed, and Billie spent long months in the hospital. However, in the sixties, after Preservation Hall opened, the Pierces began one of the most remarkable comebacks in New Orleans musical history. They have been recorded on several labels, have appeared on national television spectaculars, have toured the United States from coast to coast several times, and in 1967 toured Europe with their band.

ROBICHAUX, JOE—piano

b. March 8, 1900, New Orleans
d. January 17, 1965, New Orleans

Joe Robichaux's uncle, Professor John Robichaux, led a well-known dance orchestra. Sometimes they rehearsed at Joe's home, and by the time Joe was seven, he was interested enough to start listening to music and playing a little. When he finished high school he studied the piano style of Steve Lewis, who played with the A. J. Piron orchestra. Joe always said that Steve's playing and help were the main influences in his own development.

Joe's first real job was a tour with a tent show. In 1918 he played with trumpeter "Tig" Chambers in Chicago, and later joined Evan Thomas' Black Eagle Band of Crowley, Louisiana. Returning to New Orleans in the mid-twenties, he joined Lee Collins and Dave Jones at the Lavida dance hall. Later they moved to the Astoria, where they recorded for Victor in 1929. Some of the tunes recorded were Robichaux's own compositions.

Joe led his own band at the Entertainer's Club, and in 1932 took the band to New York, where they recorded several sides for Vocalion, including some of Joe's own numbers. In 1933 he organized a fifteen-piece band which toured the United States and Cuba. Later he worked with John Robichaux's orchestra and with Lizzie Miles, with whom he recorded in the late forties and fifties. The last eight years of his life he played piano regularly for George Lewis and with him toured Europe in 1958-59 and Japan in 1963.

At Preservation Hall Joe usually appeared with George Lewis, although he frequently worked with many of the other bands. His pleasant personality and great musical adaptability made him an ideal replacement if one of the bands needed a piano player.

Joe has been recorded so often that a list would be superfluous.

ROBINSON, NATHAN ("JIM")—trombone

b. December 25, 1892, Deer Range, La.

As a youngster Jim Robinson studied guitar but turned to the trombone while in the Army in France during World War I. After his discharge, Jim returned to New Orleans, where he worked as a longshoreman and had the opportunity to listen to bands at Economy Hall near his home. During this time he practiced trombone with his sister's player piano as accompaniment and had a few lessons from Sonny Henry. One night when Kid Rena's trombonist failed to show up at an Economy Hall dance, Jim was asked to fill in. After that he began playing with a few other bands, and about 1922 he joined the Sam Morgan band, with which he remained for several years until Sam's illness forced the group to disband about 1933. Jim was with the band when it made the famous series of Sam Morgan recordings for Columbia in 1927.

During the depression Jim worked on the docks and occasionally in bands with Kid Howard, George Lewis, and others. When a trombonist was urgently needed for Kid Rena's recording session for Delta in 1940, they found Jim Robinson sleeping on a barroom step, with his trombone on his lap, after a street parade. Jim's participation in this first "revivalist" recording led to several other engagements, and he became the most prominent trombonist in New Orleans in the period that followed. His trombone style epitomizes the "old-time sound," as he plays counter melodies to the trumpet lead and fills in rhythmic figures and "slides" in punctuating the ensembles.

Jim recorded on most of Bunk Johnson's discs of the forties and also played the 1945 and 1946 New York engagements with him. Since the mid-forties Jim has made dozens of recordings with George Lewis, with whom he toured the United States and Europe. In recent years Jim has led his own group for Atlantic, Pearl, and Riverside recordings, and was the trombonist in 1964 on the Preservation Hall Sweet Emma recording at the Tyrone Guthrie Theater in Minneapolis.

At Preservation Hall Jim has won an enthusiastic and loyal following as leader of his own band and as a member of Sweet Emma's group, Percy Humphrey's band, and others. He also toured the United States with Billie and DeDe Pierce on their college tours of 1966-67.

SAYLES, EMANUEL—banjo, guitar

b. January 31, 1905, Donaldsonville, La.

Emanuel Sayles is the son of the well-known musician, George Sayles. Emanuel first studied violin and viola under Dave Perkins, but taught himself to play the two instruments for which he is best known, the guitar and banjo.

After graduating from high school, he joined Edmond Hall's group in Pensacola, Florida, where he stayed for about two years, but then returned to New Orleans to join Ridgley's Tuxedo Orchestra. During this period he played at the Pelican dance hall, and later he was on the steamer *Capitol* with Fate Marable and on the *J. S.* with Armand J. Piron. He also played at the Roof Garden with Sidney Desvigne's orchestra, and occasionally with the Jones-Collins Astoria Hot Eight, with which he recorded in 1929 on guitar.

About 1933 Sayles went to Chicago where he played as leader of his own group and as sideman on guitar with other groups. In 1949 he again returned to New Orleans where he became the banjoist in the George Lewis band, after banjoist Lawrence Marrero's death. He accompanied the band to Japan in 1963 and 1964.

Emanuel has played at Preservation Hall as sideman with many bands and as leader of his own group. His style is brilliant and facile, and he is adaptable and easy to get along with. He sings blues vocals as well as Jelly Roll numbers and spirituals.

Emanuel has recorded on the Nobility and GHB labels, on several Southland releases, on the Riverside "Living Legends" series, and on the Atlantic "Jazz at Preservation Hall" issues. In 1964 he made trips to Disneyland and to Minneapolis with Sweet Emma Barrett, and in 1965 he returned to Chicago, replacing Mike McKendrick at Bill Reinhart's famous Jazz Limited. In 1968 he came back to New Orleans and resumed playing at Preservation Hall.

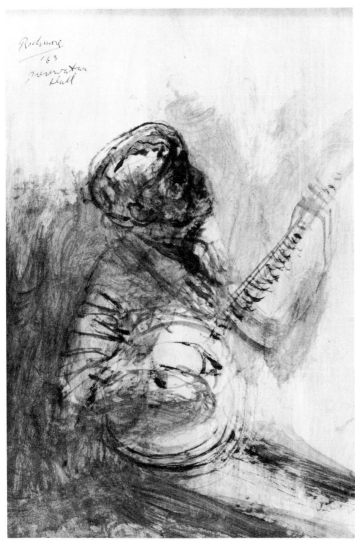

THOMAS, WORTHIA G. ("SHOW BOY")—trombone

b. February 26, 1907, Napoleonville, La.

Worthia began playing drums at fourteen and continued to play them for about twenty years. His first band job, for which he was paid $1.50, was in Napoleonville at a baseball game. It is interesting that Louis Nelson was trombonist on this job.

Worthia had four uncles who were musicians, two of whom had conservatory training and saw that musical education was available to their nephew. One of them, August Leblanch, started Worthia on trombone. At sixteen Worthia came to New Orleans and studied trombone with Professor David Jones, but he always claims that Bill Matthews was his principle teacher.

During Thomas' early years on the trombone he continued to play drums, most often as snare drummer in street parades in which he worked occasionally with Jack Carey's band. In 1929 he began traveling. His first tour was with Robert Taylor's Knee-High Revue, followed by a succession of carnivals, minstrel shows, and traveling circuses, including thirteen years with the Rabbit Foot Minstrels. In 1934 he toured with the "Miss Broadway" show out of Chicago. Later he played with John Tunkin's band in Alexandria, Louisiana, followed by six and a half years with the Jay McShane band from Kansas City. He gave up traveling shows in 1960 after a tour with the Clyde Beatty show, and has remained in New Orleans since then, appearing as a regular member of Narvin Kimball's band, and as a replacement with Paul Barbarin and many other traditional groups.

He occasionally appears at Preservation Hall with a variety of bands, and in 1967 he accompanied Kid Sheik on his tour of Japan.

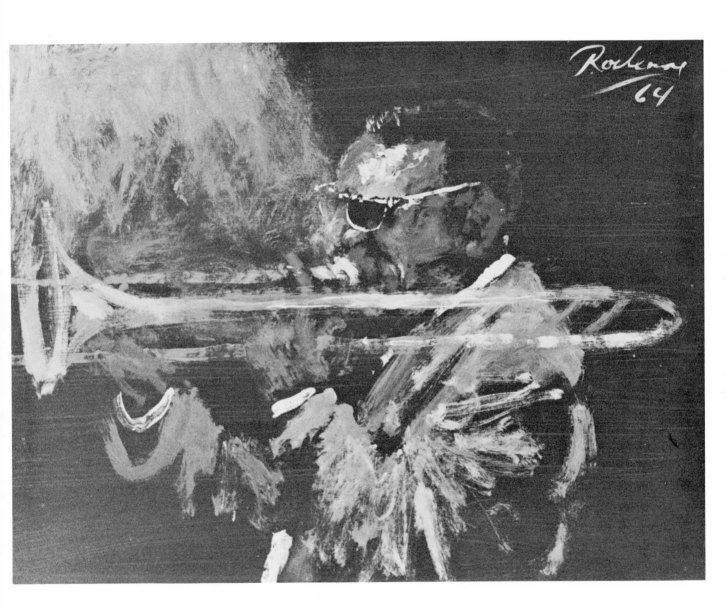

TILLMAN, WILBERT—sousaphone

b. March 31, 1898, New Orleans
d. February 11, 1967, New Orleans

Wilbert Tillman's first instrument was a clarinet. He soon switched to trumpet and then to alto sax, but finally found his real career with the tuba and string bass. He had lessons on alto sax from Fess Manetta, who also acquainted him with the New Orleans jazz idiom. His other instructors included Dave Perkins, Pinchback Touro, and Professor Chaligny.

Wilbert's first professional engagement was with the Camelia Brass Band, when he was twenty-one years old. During the following forty-five years he played with most of the New Orleans brass bands, including the Onward Brass Band led by Manuel Perez, the Young Tuxedo Brass Band, and the Eureka Brass Band. When his cousin John Casimir, leader of the Young Tuxedo Brass Band, died, Wilbert took over as leader, until 1964 when he suffered a slight stroke. This ended his parading career, but it did not diminish his love of the music. He occasionally played at Preservation Hall with Billie and DeDe Pierce and with the Young Tuxedo Band under John Casimir and under his own leadership. One of his most valuable contributions to Preservation Hall was his influence on Allan Jaffe, who has become a fine jazz tuba player.

In 1963 he made a trip to Houston to play for the Contemporary Art Festival. Musicians included Billie and DeDe Pierce, Andrew Morgan, and Albert Jiles. Tillman recorded with the Young Tuxedo Brass Band on the Atlantic release "Jazz Begins."

VALENTINE, THOMAS ("KID THOMAS")—trumpet

b. February 3, 1896, Reserve, La.

Thomas Valentine's father was a trumpeter with the Picquet Brass Band of St. John's Parish, Louisiana. He was also the instrument keeper for the band, which gave young Thomas the opportunity to practice on many different instruments. By 1915 Thomas was playing cornet in clubs across the river, and in 1923 he moved to Algiers, where he joined a five-piece band led by banjoist Elton Theodore. Within a couple of years Thomas was the leader of the band, and, because of his exciting, stomping style, he developed a loyal following. In 1936 he began playing at the Moulin Rouge, a night club with a large dance hall, and for over twenty years his group, the Kid Thomas band, was the house orchestra. Members of the band varied with the exception of Joe James, who was with the band from its beginning until his death.

In 1962 the Kid Thomas band, augmented by George Lewis, made a trip to the Minneapolis–St. Paul area. Their appearance at the new Tyrone Guthrie Theater was so well received that New Orleans bands have been making trips to the twin cities ever since. In 1964, under the aegis of Barry Martyn, Kid went to England where he recorded with several English groups. Later in the year he made the tour which played the Arkansas Arts Center, and in 1965 he made a trip to Japan with the George Lewis band.

Kid Thomas is a natural showman and has an exuberant, driving command of his instrument. His ratty tone speaks for rough New Orleans jazz. He is a disciplinarian and has his band rehearse frequently. In the early days when Preservation Hall was an art gallery, Thomas would bring his band over at night for rehearsals. The rehearsals drew such enthusiastic audiences and such generous kitty contributions that the need for a showcase for traditional New Orleans music became obvious. It is almost certain that Preservation Hall would not have evolved were it not for the vision and cooperation of Thomas Valentine.

WALTERS, ALBERT VINCENT ("FERNANDEZ")—trumpet

b. July 19, 1905—New Orleans

Albert Walters comes from a musical Creole family. Among the musicians he is better known as Albert Fernandez, since he was raised by his stepfather, Panistat Fernandez, an Indian-Creole who lived to be about 110.

Albert started in music by playing piano at house parties, and in the twenties he began working in bands with Kid Howard and later Red Allen, with whom he played for two years on Decatur Street.

While working as pianist in Wooden Joe Nicholas' Camelia Band, Fernandez took up trumpet and soon replaced Wooden Joe. He took lessons on trumpet from Professor Chaligny and Manuel Perez and gained experience in reading music while working with David Jones in a jitney dance hall job. Albert played for picnics at Milneburg and the other lake resorts, such as Spanish Fort and West End, and for many dances at most of the old-time New Orleans halls. Occasionally he played at the Last Round-Up on Bienville and Dauphine with Albert Jiles.

Fernandez has had wide experience in brass bands since about 1929, when he joined the Tulane Brass Band. He later was a regular member of George Williams' Brass Band and recorded in 1958 with Casimir's Young Tuxedo Band.

He appears from time to time at Preservation Hall, usually as a replacement for Alvin Alcorn.

WARNER, ALBERT—trombone

b. December 31, 1890, New Orleans
d. September 10, 1966, New Orleans

Albert Warner is best known as a brass band musician. In the course of his long career he played with the Excelsior Brass Band, the Columbia Brass Band, the Pacific Brass Band, the Original Tuxedo Brass Band, and for the last thirty-three years of his life with the Eureka Brass Band, as a regular member.

Albert's father was a bass player, and although Albert was always interested in music, he did not take up the trombone until he was about twenty-two years old. He took lessons from Ulysses Jackson and Honore Dutrey. His first job was in the early twenties with the Bull's Club band. He also played occasionally with many dance bands, including those of Big Eye Louis Delisle, Kid Rena, Wooden Joe Nicholas, Buddy Petit, Chris Kelly, and the Camelia band with Elmer Talbert. Albert became a regular member of the Eureka Brass Band in 1932, and when Charles Sonny Henry joined the band in 1947, he and Sonny worked out brilliant trombone passages which set the band apart from other marching bands. In 1951 Albert and Sonny were recorded with the band for Pax and in 1958 for Folkways. Shortly thereafter Sonny Henry retired from the band. In addition to his recordings with Sonny, Warner recorded with George Lewis and Bunk Johnson on Commodore in 1942, and also appeared on the Atlantic "Jazz at Preservation Hall" series in 1962.

In the early days of Preservation Hall Albert Warner appeared there frequently and also made some of the Preservation Hall tours—to Cleveland in 1961 with Kid Sheik, to Washington, D.C., in 1962 with the Eureka Brass Band, and to Memphis in 1965 with Billie and DeDe Pierce.

WATKINS, JOE—drums

b. October 24, 1900, New Orleans

Joe Watkins says that as a child he used to beat on his mother's pots and pans, her wash tub, and on wooden fences. As a teen-ager he was influenced by Baby Dodds, Zutty Singleton, Red Happy, and Black Benny. When he was nineteen or twenty, he ordered a set of real drums and took lessons from Henry Martin, but he has never learned to read music. Joe's first professional jobs were mostly house parties, until he joined the Foster Lewis band, which took jobs all over town. Then during the depression Joe played in a trio with Herb Morand on trumpet and Black Walter on guitar, but jobs became scarce, the trio broke up, and Joe had to sell his drums.

Later he bought another set of drums and began playing with George Lewis at Manny's Tavern and the El Morocco Club on Bourbon Street. In 1955 he went with Lewis to the Beverly Caverns in Los Angeles and also played at the Monterey Jazz Festival while in California. He came back to New Orleans for a while, until he was called to play at the Hangover Club in San Francisco, and from there he went back to the Beverly Caverns in Los Angeles. For the next four years he alternated between the two cities playing with Earl Hines, George Lewis, and others. During this period he went with Lewis on his first tour of Europe, and later, in 1963, he accompanied him to Japan.

Returning again to New Orleans, he played casual engagements until George Lewis began to appear regularly at Preservation Hall. At this time, in addition to playing with Lewis, Joe played for Punch Miller. Joe's style is considered typical of New Orleans drummers. Until his retirement in 1966, he was acknowledged as one of the best timekeepers in the area and was much sought after because of his many vocals. He has recorded several times, mostly with the George Lewis Band.

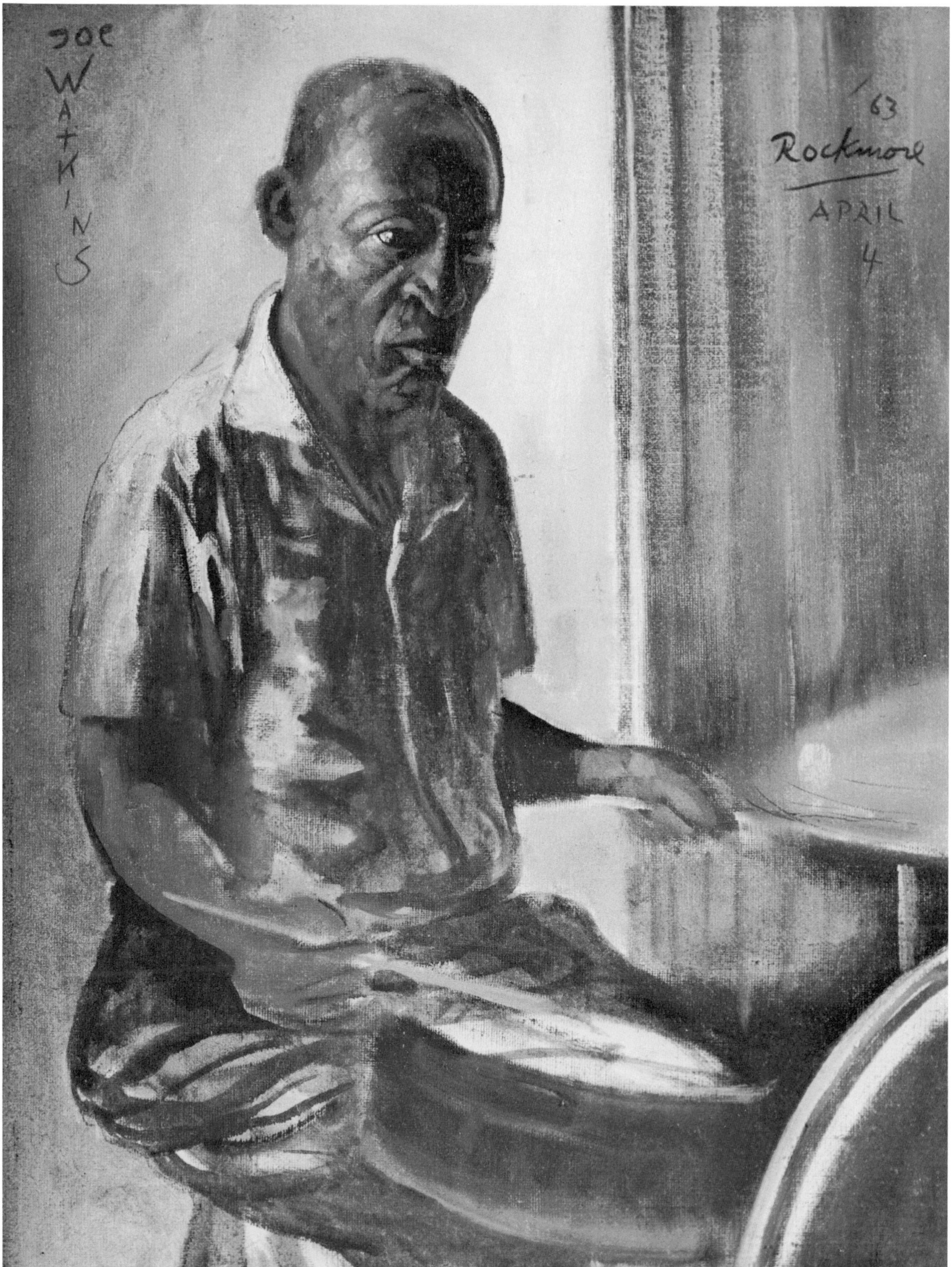
JOE WATKINS
'63
Rockmore
APRIL
4

WIGGS, JOHNNY—cornet

b. July 25, 1899, New Orleans

Johnny Wiggs was born in New Orleans as John Wiggington Hyman. His grandfather was Chief Justice of the Supreme Court of Louisiana and his uncle drafted the ordinance creating Storyville. Johnny studied violin during his teens but switched to cornet after hearing Joe Oliver play dances at the Tulane University gym. His early career was in dance bands—the New Orleans Owls, the Jung Roof Orchestra, and the Liberty Syncopators. He also played in a combo, led by Norman Brownlee, in which he replaced the legendary Emmett Hardy. In the mid-twenties he recorded with Tony Parenti on Columbia, and in 1927 he recorded with his own group, Johnny Hyman's Bayou Stompers, on Victor.

For many years he operated a music school, and his pupils include such well-known New Orleans musicians as Pete Fountain, Jack Delaney, Sid Davila, Sam Butera, and the late George Girard. A whole generation of young musicians still calls him "Professor Hyman." He is also a founder of the New Orleans Jazz Club.

His musical style was influenced by cornetists Bix Beiderbecke and Joe Oliver. There are times when his playing is reminiscent of them, although he manages to make the music his own.

Johnny has contributed much to the jazz revival of the fifties. During this period he recorded with Tom Brown for Southland and GHB and with Emile Christian for Golden Crest and Good Time Jazz. He is also known as a composer and is a member of ASCAP. Among his tunes are "Congo Square," "King Zulu Parade," "Postman's Lament," "Chef Menteur Joys," and the official march of New Orleans, "Canal Street March." In his nonmusical profession he taught architectural drawing in the New Orleans high school system for twenty-five years.

After a five-year retirement, he returned to jazz in 1965 and appeared frequently at Preservation Hall until 1967, when he retired again.

ZARDIS, CHESTER ("BEAR" or "LITTLE CHESTER")—bass

b. May 27, 1900, New Orleans

As a boy Chester Zardis and his five brothers shined shoes and sold papers to aid their mother. He got into trouble and had to spend a short time in Captain Jones's Waif's Home (now Milne Boys' Home). After his release Chester worked in a milk dairy, in a bakery, and later with a transfer company.

In 1915 he met Billie Marrero, who was playing at a banquet. Chester arranged to buy an old bass from Marrero for five dollars and to take lessons twice a week at fifty cents each. He continued to help the family, selling peanuts and working as a porter in an Annette Street movie house for six dollars a week. Eventually, he changed teachers and studied with Dave Perkins, who taught him to read music. After three years he joined the Merit Band, a neighborhood group in the Seventh Ward. He played so well that Buddy Manaday, banjo player with Buddy Petit, recommended Chester to Buddy. Petit's band, one of New Orleans' best, got many of the downtown jobs, such as advertisement gigs at the St. Bernard Market. They also had weekend jobs at Milneburg and on the steamer *Camelia* excursions. Later the band relocated in Covington and played in the towns across Lake Pontchartrain for about four years.

In 1925 Chester returned to New Orleans to play with Kid Rena, and after a couple of years he played with Chris Kelly, Jack Carey, Kid Clayton, and Kid Howard. He also played with Walter Pichon on the riverboat *Capitol* and with the Black Eagle Band of Crowley, Louisiana. In 1942 and 1943 he recorded with Bunk Johnson and George Lewis, and then after service in World War II, he played with bands in Denver and Philadelphia, before joining Herb Morand on the Mississippi Gulf Coast.

Chester returned to Louisiana in the early sixties, and in 1964 he wrote to George Lewis, who was playing at Preservation Hall, and asked if George needed him. Then in 1965 he joined Lewis' band. He plays frequently with Billie and DeDe Pierce and recorded with them in 1966 on the Preservation Hall label. The following year, in 1967, he accompanied Kid Sheik on his tour of Japan.

THE

EUREKA

BRASS

BAND

The Eureka Brass Band, the most widely known of the remaining New Orleans brass bands, has been closely associated with Preservation Hall. Almost all of the Eureka bandmen have played in the Hall as members of various small groups. In the fall of 1961 Preservation Hall sponsored a series of Sunday afternoon parades in which the band marched through the French Quarter and then gave a two-hour concert.

The Eureka has paraded as an organized group for more than forty-five years, and some of the city's outstanding jazzmen have been members. The founders of the band, Willie Wilson and Alcide Landry, considered it to be the lodge band of the Hobgoblin Club, but when the band started getting outside bookings, including jobs from the Odd Fellows Lodge, the name changed to the Eureka Brass Band. About 1935, when Wilson was stricken with a heart attack during a parade, T-Boy Remy assumed leadership, and shortly thereafter Percy Humphrey, the present leader, joined the band.

The Eureka has developed a distinctive musical style and a repertoire of unusual numbers. To avoid being imitated the titles were cut off the band parts, and the tunes were identified only by numbers. For example, the leader might say "No. 9," and the musicians, playing from titleless sheets, would perform an inimitable dirge. Intermingled with these exclusive renditions are the traditional hymns such as "Gloryland," "Just a Little While to Stay Here," "Take Your Burden to the Lord," and, of course, "The Saints." Another feature is the selection of happy numbers played after the departure from the cemetery. "Didn't He Ramble" and "Down in Honkytonk Town" were traditional choices, but Percy Humphrey, with tongue in cheek, has been known to call for "Lady Be Good," "Who's Sorry Now?" and, on at least one occasion, "I'll Be Glad When You're Dead, You Rascal You."

Among the jobs the band has played have been christenings, advertising engagements, picnics, dances, weddings, television commercials, cornerstone layings, social club functions, and more somber occasions, such as candlelight memorial services and funeral processions. It has also performed at depots and airports for the arrival and departure of notables, and in the Mardi Gras parades for such contrasting organizations as Zulu and Rex.

It was not until 1962 that the Eureka Brass Band was heard outside New Orleans. Parading on the streets of Washington, D.C., at the First International Jazz Festival, the band was the hit of the show. It has been recorded several times: in 1951 on Pax, in 1958 on Folkways, and in 1962 as part of Atlantic's "Jazz at Preservation Hall" series.

Fats Houston

Percy Humphrey

Members of the band whose biographical sketches appear in the book are Percy Humphrey, Willie Humphrey, "Slow Drag" Pavageau, Wilbert Tillman, Peter Bocage, Cie Frazier, Chicken Henry, Kid Shiek (Cola), and Emanuel Paul. Other members, whose pictures appear in this section, are the following:

Albert Warner

Kid Sheik

Chicken Henry

Cie Frazier

MATTHEW "FATS" HOUSTON, widely known as a grand marshal with the Eureka Brass Band and other bands, has had extensive experience as a dance band drummer. In the forties he led several dance bands. He has worked with many jazz musicians, including Sweet Emma, Kid Howard, Bill Matthews, and George Guesnon.

HENRY "BOOKER T." GLASS is a drummer with the Eureka Brass Band. He has been playing in New Orleans brass bands since the early thirties, starting with Wooden Joe Nicholas' Camelia Band. He has also played with jazz and dance bands. In the forties he played at the De Soto Tavern with Albert Walters, John Smith, and Louis Nelson.

ROBERT LEWIS, otherwise known as "Son Few Clothes," was one of Louis Armstrong's childhood pals and a fellow resident of Captain Jones's Waif's Home (now called Milne Boys' Home). He started to play bass drum in marching bands in the early twenties, and joined the Eureka Brass Band in 1939.

HENRY CLARENCE "SHANK" WILLIAMS was a grand marshal with the Eureka Band and other brass bands, until his death December 30, 1965. For many years, in his role as grand marshal for the Young and True Friends Benevolent Association and for the Eagles Aid and Pleasure Club, Shank was often seen leading a sorrowful procession through the streets of New Orleans. When his own turn came for the closer walk, the streets of the Carrollton section were lined with club members, church groups, and his own progeny, who included seventeen grandchildren and twenty-five great-grandchildren. It seems appropriate that the Eureka Brass Band, which Shank had led on countless similar occasions, should play for his final journey. As the body was carried out of the church, the band broke into "Just a Little While to Stay Here," and as they continued with "What a Friend We Have in Jesus," the skies opened and a torrential downpour silenced the ritual—a fitting symbolic finale.

Robert "Son Few Clothes" Lewis

Booker T. Glass

Slow Drag Pavageau

Shank Williams

MISCELLANY

Louis Nelson, DeDe and Billie Pierce

George Lewis

Chicken Henry

Punch Miller and Louis Nelson

Andrew Morgan and Louis Nelson

Louis Nelson, Joe Watkins, Punch Miller, Papa John Joseph, George Lewis, and Dolly Adams

Jim Robinson and Ernie Cagnolatti

Israel Gorman and Joseph Butler

Jim Robinson

Louis Nelson, Kid Thomas, and Emanuel Paul

Ernie Cagnolatti, Willie Humphrey, and Sweet Emma

Jim Robinson, Punch Miller, and George Lewis

Jim Robinson, Joe Watkins, and George Lewis

Mother Margaret Parker, a gospel singer

ROCKMORE

BORENSTEIN

RUSSELL

A Publisher's Note

NOEL ROCKMORE

Noel Rockmore was born in New York City in 1928, the son of two well-known artists, Gladys Rockmore Davis and Floyd Davis. As a youth Noel was a promising musician, but an early illness forced him to abandon thoughts of a musical career.

His paintings have been exhibited at the Metropolitan Museum of Art, Whitney Museum, and the Museum of Modern Art. He has had many one-man shows and has won a number of awards, including the Hallgarten Prize and the Wallace Truman Prize, both awarded by the National Academy. He has also been the recipient of a Tupperware Fellowship, a Tiffany Fellowship, and an artist-in-residence grant from the Ford Foundation. His paintings have received considerable attention, including a two-page color spread in *Life*. Paintings from his Preservation Hall series are on display in the Hall and in the Touché Bar of the Royal Orleans Hotel. A number of them have found their way into prominent public and private collections.

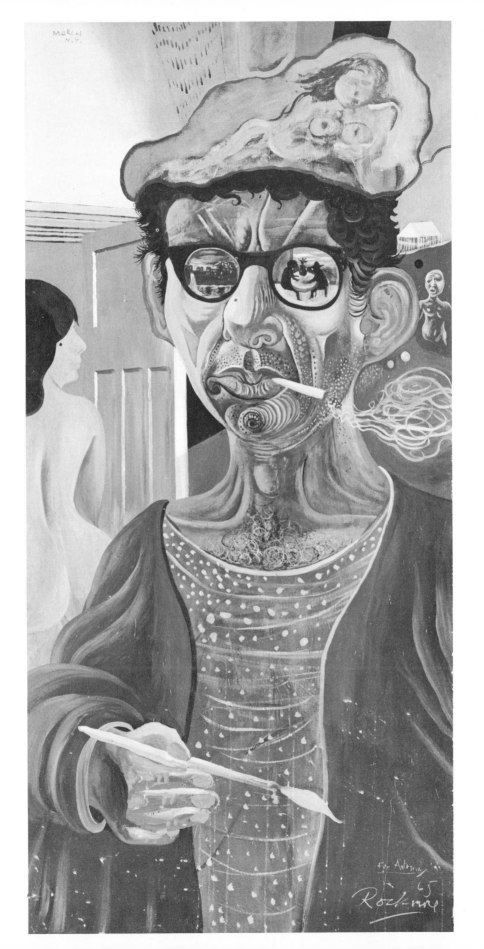

E. LORENZ BORENSTEIN

Larry Borenstein was born in Milwaukee in 1919. His father played baritone horn in a Russian Army band stationed at Riga, Latvia. Larry left home at fifteen to work in the "Streets of Paris" show at the Chicago World's Fair. For several years he toured with a variety of circuses and carnivals doing legerdemain and illusions. He settled in New Orleans in 1941, and has operated a succession of French Quarter shops catering to collectors of stamps, coins, rare books, documents, paintings, and pre-Columbian artifacts. In the early fifties he published the *Old French Quarter News*, a weekly tabloid.

Although Borenstein played the drums briefly as a child, his only claim to musical fame is that he is the only Jewish Scotch bagpiper in the French Quarter. He learned to play in the fifties under the tutelage of Pipe Major Roy Chapman of the Royal Canadian Highlanders.

BILL RUSSELL

Bill Russell is generally acknowledged to be one of the leading authorities on New Orleans jazz. He was born in February, 1905, in Canton, Missouri. He graduated from the Quincy, Illinois, Conservatory of Music but went on to study science in college. He did graduate work in music at Teachers College, Columbia University, and at UCLA under Arnold Schoenberg. His compositions for percussion groups have been published and recorded. During the depression he taught music in New York, and for six years he toured the country as a member of the Red Gate Shadow Players, furnishing the musical accompaniment on authentic Chinese instruments.

In the late thirties Russell began writing articles for some of the small jazz magazines. In 1939 he wrote three chapters for *Jazzmen*, one of the first American books on jazz, and two years later co-edited the *Jazz Record Book*. In 1942 he started recording musicians in New Orleans, including Bunk Johnson, for his "American Music" label. In all, more than sixty records were released, all of them now collector's items. In 1958, when Tulane University received a Ford Foundation grant for an archive of New Orleans jazz, Russell was appointed curator.